JACK AND THE BEANSTALK

A pantomime

by Chris Denys and Chris Harris

JOSEF WEINBERGER PLAYS

LONDON

Jack and the Beanstalk
First published in 2002
by Josef Weinberger Ltd
12-14 Mortimer Street, London, W1T 3JJ

ISBN 0 85676 255 5

Printed by Watkiss Studios Ltd, Biggleswade, Beds.

This Pantomime of **JACK AND THE BEANSTALK** was first produced by the Bristol Old Vic Company at the Theatre Royal, Bristol on December 1st 1994 with the following cast:

Sir Beastly de Bedminster	Cliff Howells
Fairy Blodwen of Builth Wells	Dariel Pertwee
King Athelred the Unsteady	Ian Saunders
Princess Katherine	Jenny Coulston
Simple Simon	Patrick Miller
Jack Durdham	Anna Rose
Dame Dolabella Durdham	Chris Harris
Daisy, the Cow	Aubrey Budd *With either* Lucy McKerron *or* Kay Thomas
Giant Blunderbore	Aubrey Budd
Queen of the Doves	Jo Pollicutt *or* Alice Sara
The Magic Harp	Lisa Rae *or* Natalie Herbert
Villagers, Doves, Ravens, Ghosts	The Dancers of Acrodance 2000

Directed by Chris Denys
Designed by Mick Bearwish
Music Directed by John O'Hara
Music Supervised by Neil Rhoden
Choreography by Gail Gordon
Lighting Designed by Tim Streader
Sound Designed by Mark Gallagher

When revived in 1999 and for the subsequent transfer to Cheltenham in 2000 and this publication, King Aethelred became Squire Allgood and Princess Katherine became his horsey daughter Kate. Dame Dolabella Durdham became Dame Letitia Lansdown, Jack Durdham became Jack Lansdown and the Doves disappeared, leaving the Ravens triumphant.

CHARACTERS

(In order of their appearance)

SIR BEASTLY DE BEDMINSTER	*A black-hearted knight*
FAIRY BLODWEN OF BUILTH WELLS	*A very good Welsh Fairy*
SQUIRE ALLGOOD	
KATE ALLGOOD	*His Daughter*
SIMPLE SIMON	
JACK LANSDOWN	*The Hero*
DAME LETITIA LANDSOWN	*His Mother*
DAISY THE COW	
GIANT BLUNDERBORE	

CHORUS *as* VILLAGERS, BEAN FAIRIES, RAVENS, GHOSTS

SCENES

ACT ONE

Scene 1: IN FRONT OF PANTO GAUZE
Scene 2: THE VILLAGE GREEN – OUTSIDE DAME LANDSDOWN'S COTTAGE

"Journey" Transformation to:

Scene 3: THE ROAD TO MARKET
Scene 4: A CLEARING IN THE WOODS
Scene 5: INSIDE DAME LANSDOWN'S COTTAGE
Scene 6: DAME LANSDOWN'S GARDEN (*With Fully Grown Beanstalk*)

Interval

ACT TWO

Scene 1: THE TOP OF THE BEANSTALK – ABOVE THE CLOUDS
Scene 2: OUTSIDE CASTLE BLUNDERBORE
Scene 3: A CORRIDOR IN CASTLE BLUNDERBORE
Scene 4: THE KITCHEN OF CASTLE BLUNDERBORE
Scene 5: THE SAME CORRIDOR IN CASTLE BLUNDERBORE
Scene 6: DAME LANSDOWN'S GARDEN (*The foot of the Beanstalk*)
Scene 7: A CLEARING IN THE WOODS
Scene 8: WALKDOWN

AUTHORS' NOTE

This Pantomime is intended to be "traditional" in that the Principal Boy is a girl, the Dame is a man, the story is told clearly with as much action and knock-about as possible and, very importantly, it is local to the town or city in which it is performed. It's also meant to be great fun – both for the audience and for those who perform and present it.

The local references in this script relate to Cheltenham – where it was produced in 2000, the year after its second showing in Bristol. Dame Lansdown is only called Dame Lansdown because Lansdown is a district of Cheltenham (in Bristol, she was called Dame Durdham) and the same goes for Sir Beastly de Battledown (in Bristol "de Bedminster") so please feel free to localise as necessary and desirable.

Also, the staging is as described because we were working in beautifully equipped theatres with excellent design and production departments able to give us anything we asked for. It doesn't have to be like that, of course, and can be adapted to how much – or how little – you have at your disposal.

The stage directions, groundplans and indicated lighting, sound, follow-spot and pyrotechnic cues are only intended as suggestions and not to be in any way prescriptive.

The only sort of "flash" units allowed by Fire Officers these days are ruinously expensive and we always wrote our scripts with a liberal use of these effects only to cut them back to essentials when we saw what it was going to cost.

Also, there are lots of ways of creating giants but one device which helped our very splendid Blunderbore was a pair of plasterer's stilts which were surprisingly easy to master and which gave him an extra three feet of height before the top part was added.

The Music:
Pantomime audiences do like to know the tunes so we have always used either current and perennial favourites as written or taken well-known melodies and written lyrics which stand as part of the plot and move the story along.

Some of the music we have used is out of copyright (eg: the Act One Finale is set to the "Miserere from Verdi's "Il Trovatore" and is clear) *but other melodies are still* ***in*** *copyright and you will need to pay for these if you use them through the* ***Performing Rights Society*** (who offer a special deal for Pantomimes).

Mostly, though, we have found that producers prefer to choose their own music to suit and show off the particular voices of their cast.

ACT ONE

Music: Overture.

At the end of the Overture, there is a Crash of Thunder. ***(SQ.1; LXQ.1; FSQ.1)***

Scene One

Before the Panto Gauze.

SIR BEASTLY is revealed, muffled in his cloak, his back to the AUDIENCE. He turns slowly and smiles an evil smile.

SIR BEASTLY: *(ingratiating)* Good people, good day. I'm delighted to meet ye . . .
Nay, zounds . . . fear me not, pray. Sir Beastly won't eat ye!
Gadzooks, we'll be butties if only you're willin'
For I am your friendly neighbourhood VILLAIN!
Don't hiss me, nay!
Don't boo, I pray.
Odds bodkins, don't be nervous –
You'll find I'm quite
A delightful knight –
Sir Beastly de Battledown – at your service.
I can tell from your looks
You're a fine bunch of crooks –
Fit friends for a black-hearted knight.
And I'll give you a fractional
Share of the action –
If only you play your cards right.
So how do you feel then?
Is it a deal then?
Be my comrades while I do my worst?
And I will reward you
'Cos I can afford to
When I am – King Beastly the First!

(There is a Flash – ***(PyroQ.1; LXQ.2; FSQ.2)*** *and FAIRY BLODWEN appears DR.)*

BLODWEN: Oh no you won't.

SIR BEASTLY: Oh yes I will.

BLODWEN: *(leading the AUDIENCE)* Oh no you won't!

SIR BEASTLY: Oh yes I will!

BLODWEN: Oh no you won't. Well, there's a sauce!
You know you're banned
From this pleasant land,
You nasty knight, now on your horse.
(Seeing the AUDIENCE.) Oh . . . There's lovely . . . Oh
. . . Hello! *(Moving DR.)*
I'm Fairy Blodwen of Builth Wells, you know.
Croeso i Pantomime, bechgyn a genethod, my dears
Take no notice of the nasty knight.
Fairy Blodwen'll box his ears.

SIR BEASTLY: Ignore the fey. Stick with Beastly, I say.
Are you with me?

BLODWEN: Be with Blodwen!

SIR BEASTLY: Will you do it?

AUDIENCE: NO.

SIR BEASTLY: Then remember one thing,
When I'm Charlton's King –
I gave you your chance – and you blew it.

BLODWEN: You cheeky thing!
We want no king!
On that we're most emphatic.
It's the people who'll
Decide who'll rule.
We're completely democratic!

SIR BEASTLY: Oh, King I'll be –
Just wait and see –
What horror I've got in store!
You'll all leave town
When I bring down –
My mate – the Giant – BLUNDERBORE!

(There is a crash of Thunder.) ***(SQ.2.)***

BLODWEN: *(horrified)* Blunderbore!?!

SIR BEASTLY: He's gurt, he's vast.

You'll be aghast.
You'll scuttle off like rabbits
He's about as tall
As Cheltenham Town Hall
With some very nasty habits.

BLODWEN: I command you cease!
This land's at peace
And nothing shall disturb it.
(Rhapsodic.) This sceptered isle –
This land of smiles . . .

SIR BEASTLY: Oh, shut up, you small Welsh rarebit!

BLODWEN: Blunderbore
May rant and roar
And thunder with his feet –
But he's up there
And we're down yer
And never the twain shall meet.

SIR BEASTLY: That's what you think,
You fairy . . . fink,
But I've these magic beans.
And Sir Beastly's got a beastly plot.

BLODWEN: I wonder what he means?
But . . . just a minute!
Them's my beans, innit?
You stole them beans from me!

SIR BEASTLY: I'll not excuse it.
You should lock it or lose it!

BLODWEN: Well, you . . . proper mochyn du! *(Pronounced – almost – dee.)*
But you'll come to grief,
You evil thief,
For stealing beans means fines.

SIR BEASTLY: That's where you're odd then,
Fairy Blodwen.
As we all know – *(Leading the AUDIENCE.)*
Beanz – meanz – Heinz.

BLODWEN: You're vile, you're yucky . . .

SIR BEASTLY: Now listen, ducky,

You'll find I'm mean and tricksy . . .

BLODWEN: There's nasty you are . . .

SIR BEASTLY: Don't go too far
You naff Taff Celtic pixie!
These beans'll sprout
A stem so stout
The Giant will clamber down,
Then he'll have this bunch
For his Sunday lunch
And devastate the town!

(A Crash of Thunder. ***(SQ.1)*** *SIR BEASTLY sweeps off DL, cackling nastily.)* ***(LXQ.3; FSQ.1A)***

BLODWEN: Well, what a rotter!
And I've not gotta
Clue what's best to do.
If Blunderbore
Comes down once more
He'll eat up me and you.
I'll see if I can
Devise a plan,
So just you relax and sit still,
And while I go
You can say hello
To the poor ragged peasants of Pittville!

(A Flash ***(Pyro Q.2; LXQ.4; FSQ.2A)*** *and she disappears DR. Musical Intro as the lights come up behind the gauze to reveal:)*

Scene Two

The Village Green. Outside DAME LANSDOWN'S Cottage.

The Gauze Flies out. ***(Fly Q.1; LXQ.5; FSQ.3)***

Song: WAKE UP AND HEAR – THE BELLS ARE RINGING *(KATE, SQUIRE and VILLAGERS)*

WAKE UP AND HEAR – THE BELLS ARE RINGING;
BIRDS ARE SINGING:
"FAREWELL SKIES OF GREY!"
DON'T WASTE TIME DREAMING YOUR LIFE AWAY –
THE SUN IS BEAMING,

IT'S THE FIRST OF MAY.
EVERY BOY
AND GIRL IS BRIMFUL OF JOY
SO LISTEN WHEN WE SAY:
"HEY!"
WAKE UP AND HEAR THE BELLS ARE RINGING
ON THIS FINE MAY DAY HOLIDAY.

(FSQ.3A)

(SIMPLE SIMON enters UL. He has his favourite (large) fluffy Bunny in a child's rucksack on his back.)

SIMON: Hello, everybody!

ALL: Hello, Simon . . .

SIMON: Say hello to Bunny!

ALL: Hello, Bunny!

BUNNY: SQUEAK!

KATE: *(to L of him)* Isn't it a spiffing day?

SIMON: Yes. The sun is shining, the birds are singing, the hedgehogs are playing leapfrog.

SQUIRE: *(to R of him)* How does a hedgehog play leapfrog?

SIMON: Very carefully.

(*All laugh.*)

KATE: Have you seen Jack?

SIMON: Oh, him! He's meandering up on Marle Hill – dreaming as usual.

KATE: Dreaming? *(Moves DC, sings:)* ***(FSQ.4)***
THE ONE I LOVE SPENDS ALL HIS LIFE IN
DAYDREAMS.
HE DOESN'T SEEM TO CARE FOR ME AT ALL.

SIMON, SQUIRE & VILLAGERS: NOT AT ALL?

KATE: IF ONLY, SOMETIMES HE
WOULD NOTICE ME . . .

SIMON, SQUIRE & VILLAGERS: BUT YOU KNOW HE LOVES
YOU BEST OF ALL!
SO!

(FSQ.4A)

ALL: WAKE UP AND HEAR *(Etc.)*

(FSQ.4B)

(JACK enters UL in a dream.)

SIMON: Look out! *(LC.)* Here he comes now.

KATE: *(to L of him)* Hello, Jack.

SQUIRE: *(to R of him)* Jack?

VILLAGERS: JACK!

JACK: *(jumps)* What? Oh, sorry, Squire . . . I was dreaming . . .

SQUIRE: We could see that. Shouldn't you be at work, you young neer-do-well?

JACK: But, oh, Squire – work takes up too much of my spare time.

SIMON: He's so lazy even his nose won't run.

KATE: But there must be *some* job you'd enjoy. What would you *like* to be?

JACK: A hero . . .

SIMON, SQUIRE & VILLAGERS: *(ridiculing)* A hero?

(FSQ.5)

JACK: *(moving DC, sings)* I DREAM ONE DAY THAT I WILL
BE A HERO –
THE CHAMPION WHO WILL SET OUR COUNTRY FREE.

SIMON, SQUIRE & VILLAGERS: GET HE!

JACK: WHEN I'VE SEALED THE GIANT'S FATE,
I'LL ASK YOU, KATE,
IF YOU WOULD EVER MARRY ME?

KATE: YES!

(FSQ.5A; LXQ.6)

ALL: HURRAY! SO!
WAKE UP AND HEAR, THE BELLS ARE RINGING *(Etc, to finish.)*

(FSQ.5B; LXQ.7)

BLUNDERBORE: *(from above)* FEE FI FO FUM . . . ! ***(SQ.4.)***

SIMON: *(break DL)* Look out! All this singing and dancing and bell ringing has woken Blunderbore.

SQUIRE: *(tiptoeing R)* We'd better go on the old tippy-toe, egad – jolly quietly . . .

SIMON: *(tiptoeing across to DR)* Not make a sound . . .

(Everybody tiptoes about.)

JACK: *(C – shouting upwards)* Come on then, Blunderbore. Come down here and fight!

SIMON: *(runs to R of him, hitting him)* Sssshhh!

SQUIRE: *(to R of Simon)* I say, steady!

KATE: *(to L of JACK)* Don't upset him.

JACK: *(defiant to the sky)* Come on! Coward . . .

SIMON: *(shaking him)* He don't like it.

JACK: I'm not afraid of him. One of these days, Blunderbore . . .

(A huge rock drops out of the flies ***(SQ.5)****, narrowly missing JACK and SIMON.)*

SIMON: I told you he didn't like it.

JACK: If only I could find a way to climb up to where the Giant lives.

SQUIRE: *(crossing below SIMON to R of JACK)* Jack, lad, are ye mad? Ye'll never be a hero like your Dad!

JACK: But he can't go on pestering us like this.

(SIMON kneels to tie his shoe.)

SQUIRE: Only think how much worse it used to be.

JACK: How could it be worse?

SQUIRE: Surely you know
That, long ago –
Before we had mobile phones –
The giant could invade
The Regent Arcade
Down a staircase of gurt big stones.

(BLUNDERBORE roars.) ***(SQ.6.)***

SQUIRE: Though you find his roaring
Rather boring . . .

(Another boulder drops out of the flies ***(SQ.7.)*** *and narrowly misses him.)*

SQUIRE: . . . and these rocks that he keeps dropping –
Imagine then
What it was like when
He came down every day – *(Sits on SIMON'S knee.)* – shopping.
He ate our cattle in huge cow pies –
He ate our sheep and the pigs in their styes –
He smashed all the cash from the banks' dispensers
And emptied the Food Hall at Marks and Spencers.
He robbed all the shops with a speed bewilderin'
And sometimes he even ate . . . the children . . .

ALL: SCREAM.

SQUIRE: He stole our hen that laid eggs of gold –
He ravaged all our crops.
And he stole our lovely magic harp –
that played all the Top of the Pops.

ALL: *(shouting)* SHAME, DISGUSTING! *(Etc.)*

SQUIRE: *(rising, going to JACK; SIMON falls over)*
'Til Long Larry Lansdown, your Dad, lad, egad! –
Took his blacksmith's hammer – some say he was mad –

SIMON: He *was* mad . . .

SQUIRE: But he faced the giant –
Stern and defiant –
And he smashed the stone steps down –
So Blunderbore
Could descend no more,
To terrorise the Town.

ALL: CHEER.

SQUIRE: *(tragic)* But poor Long Larry,
Chose to tarry
As that mighty staircase sank –
And the rocks fell splat!
And crushed him flat! –
He was always thick as a plank.

ALL: AAAW!

SQUIRE: It's such a shame
You're not the same –
Though a handsome little yob
But you've not enough
Of this hero stuff.
So it's time you got a job.

JACK: There's only one job for me – to fight the giant and defeat him single-handed – avenge my father, restore our fortunes – then I'd be a hero. *(Taking her hands.)* Then I could marry Kate.

KATE: Oh yes, Jack!

SQUIRE: What? *(Moving between them, pushing them apart.)* Marry me daughter? The daughter of a squire is somewhat higher than to what you can aspire. Kate must marry into the horsey set – I mean look at the girl . . .

JACK/SIMON: I'm looking. *(JACK hits SIMON.)*

SQUIRE: Did you ever see a finer filly? *(KATE mimes a rising trot.)* She's the Belle of Badminton – the pearl of the Polo Club – the dolly of dressage – got a wonderful seat.

SIMON: I'll say.

JACK: But – if I was a hero?

SQUIRE: In that unlikely event, I *might* consider it.

JACK: Then that's what I'll be. I'm not afraid of the giant, Kate.

(There is a huge roar from BLUNDERBORE.) ***(SQ.8)***

SIMON: No but you're scared stiff of your Mother and here comes Dame Lansdown now.

JACK: Mother? Oh no . . .

(They all run off R as:)

(DAME'S entrance Music. ***(LXQ.8)*** *DAME LANSDOWN enters at speed from UL in a milkmaid's outfit, wearing a yoke to which are attached two milking pails. From one of the pails, a cat's tail pokes out through a knot-hole in the side. This is motorised and spins when she presses a remote switch.)*

DAME L: *(to AUDIENCE)* Hello, you tinkers. Dame Lansdown here – Dame Letitia Lansdown of great renown – One stocking up – one stocking down – just one cow and two acres of grass . . . And a milking stool to rest my . . . now where did that go? *(She turns round revealing a three-legged milking stool velcroed onto her bottom.)*

AUDIENCE: BEHIND YOU . . . ON YOUR BOTTOM . . . *(Etc.)*

DAME L: Oh, there it is . . . *(Takes it off and throws it offstage.)* I shall need that later . . . But I'm very sad. I'm in despair. I've lost my little pussy and I don't know where. Has anybody seen my pussycat?

(The tail spins.)

AUDIENCE: IN THE BUCKET.

DAME L: *(looking in the wrong bucket)* In the bucket? She is not in the bucket.

(The tail spins.)

AUDIENCE: IN THE OTHER BUCKET. IN THE OTHER HAND. ON YOUR LEFT . . .

DAME L: In the other hand? On the left? Alright. I'll look in the other bucket. *(Turns round and looks to her R – still the wrong bucket.)* No. She isn't there either . . . *(Finding her.)* Oh here she is – slurping up the milk. She's drunk all the milk and now she's so fat she's stuck. *(Taking the prop off and handing it offstage L.)* Let's just put her over here so she doesn't get an upset tummy. There now. *(Returning to C.)* Oh, just look at me. Just a poor old widow-woman. I'm so poor . . .

AUDIENCE: Aaaaw . . .

DAME L: Oh, I'm much poorer than that . . .

AUDIENCE: AAAW!

DAME L: And I've not been well. I went to see Doctor Sluggett. He told me to drink a glass of milk after a hot bath. That was three weeks ago, and I'm still drinking the hot bath. Life's not much as a widow. Since my husband – Long Larry – passed over. Mind, I did think about marrying again. I actually advertised for a husband in the *Echo* – got hundreds of replies . . . all from women saying "You can have mine. You can have mine". But men are all alike, aren't they? Well, men are all I like anyway. And I have a million dollar figure. Who said "all in loose change?" I'll have you know my measurements are 38-24-37 – though not necessarily in that order. But, oh . . . I just can't keep up the mortgage, you see. And that Jack's worse than useless idle – bone idle. Can't get a job. Says he's on this restart – needs more of a jump start.

BLUNDERBORE: FEE FI FO FUM. ***(SQ.9)***

DAME L: Shut your mouth or I'll smack your bum!

BLUNDERBORE: BE HE ALIVE OR BE HE DEAD . . . ***(SQ.10)***

DAME L: Finish your cocoa and go to bed!

(A roar from the GIANT. A huge boulder is thrown down.) ***(SQ.11)***

DAME L: He don't half drop big 'uns. And he's so rude! But what does it matter because . . .

(FSQ.6; LXQ.9)

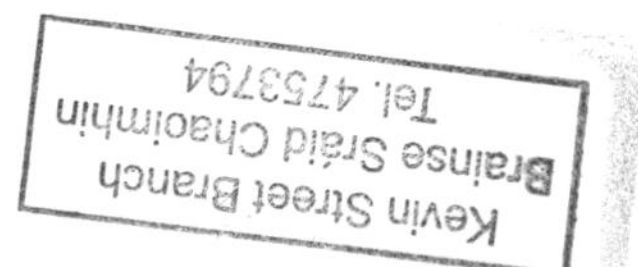

INTRO: REACH FOR THE STARS – *(or whatever is the currently popular number) DAME sings, leading SIMON and CHILDREN'S CHORUS – end of song:*

(LXQ.10; FSQ.6A)

DAME L: Right. The Milky Bars are on me!

(The VILLAGERS rush off L taking the rocks and cheering. DAME LANSDOWN tiptoes off R. There is a roar from BLUNDERBORE.) ***(SQ.12)***

(JACK enters UL to DC.)

JACK: What can I do? We all live in terror of Giant Blunderbore and all I want to do is to climb up there and fight him – man to giant – and save everybody and be a hero and marry Kate and . . .

(Flash. ***(Pyro Q.3; FSQ.7; LXQ.11)*** *FAIRY BLODWEN appears DR.)*

BLODWEN: Fear not, Jack, for you shall be
Ever famous in Cheltenham's history.

JACK: But . . . who are you?

BLODWEN: Fairy Blodwen, of Builth – guardian fairy of Cheltenham Spa.

JACK: Cheltenham certainly needs a guardian fairy just now. But you're Welsh.

BLODWEN: All fairies are Welsh, bach. It's a Celtic racket.
So you want to be a hero? Think you can hack it?

(KATE, SIMON and the VILLAGERS enter DL. They all carry towels and some are dressed for swimming. SIMON wears a striped, baggy swimsuit, plastic bathing hat and a snorkel. None of them can see the FAIRY.)

KATE: Hello, Jack . . .

JACK: *(to BLODWEN)* What?

KATE: I said "Hello Jack" . . .

BLODWEN: You're just the lad that I've been seekin'

To baffle Beastly in a manner of speakin'

JACK: *(to BLODWEN)* But what do you want with me?

KATE: *(to JACK)* To take you for a swim . . .

SIMON: *(to JACK)* Down the Lido, Jack.

BLODWEN: You're not a coward are you?

JACK: *(to BLODWEN, angrily)* No!

SIMON: *(hurt)* Alright, alright . . .

KATE: *(upset)* There's no need to be rude.

BLODWEN: Well, your people need a hero. Will you do it?

JACK: I'll do it.

SIMON: Make your mind up.

BLODWEN: You're sure you won't be afraid?

JACK: I told you I *won't* . . .

KATE: *(to Simon) I* think his mind's wandering.

SIMON: Don't worry. It's too weak to go very far.

KATE: *(to JACK)* What on earth's the matter with you?

JACK: *(to BLODWEN)* I may not look very brave but I'm not afraid of anything.

SIMON: *(to KATE)* Who's he talking to?

(KATE and SIMON wander round JACK to find out who he's talking to but can't see BLODWEN.)

JACK: I want to be a hero – more than anything in the world.

SIMON: Who're you talking to, Jack?

JACK: The fairy.

SIMON: Oh dear!

JACK: *(to BLODWEN)* But I haven't even got a sword.

KATE: What fairy?

JACK: *(pointing at BLODWEN)* That fairy.

BLODWEN: Then I'll have to get you a sword – a magic sword.

JACK: A magic sword?

SIMON: What's he on about?

KATE: Jack, dear . . . *(Feeling his forehead.)* There's no fairy . . .

SIMON: There's no fairy, Jack . . .

VILLAGERS: No fairy . . . *(Worried – to each other.)* He's seeing fairies now! He's really flipped this time . . . *(Etc.)*

BLODWEN: And then you can defeat the giant . . .

KATE: *(to JACK)* I think you'd better lie down . . .

JACK: But how? Tell me what to do . . .

SIMON: *(demonstrating, lying down)* It's dead easy. You just . . .

(LXQ.12; FSQ.7A)

Song: THE MAGIC SWORD *(JACK, BLODWEN, KATE, SIMON and VILLAGERS)*

JACK: *(stepping over SIMON to C)* HOW CAN I BE A HERO
BOLD AND WIN THE HAND OF LOVELY KATE?

BLODWEN: I TELL YOU, BACH, IT IS FORETOLD – IF BRAVE
ENOUGH IT WILL BE YOUR FATE.
THE LETHAL MATCH I HAVE IN STORE
IS TO DESPATCH OLD BLUNDERBORE
YES THAT FILTHY NASTY SMELLY BLUNDERBORE

KATE, SIMON/ VILLAGERS: IT'S VERY SAD
NOW JACK HAS GONE RIGHT OFF HIS TROLLEY
AND HAS TURNED INTO A WALLY
'COS HE SAYS HE'S SEEING FAIRIES AND SOME OTHER SILLY TALES
NOW WE SHOULD TRY TO HELP OUR FRIEND
AND GET HIM BACK UPON THE RAILS.

JACK: WE ARE SO POOR, I CANNOT AFFORD TO BUY FOR MYSELF A TRUSTY BLADE

BLODWEN: I'LL CONJURE YOU A MAGIC SWORD TO AID YOU IN YOUR PERILOUS CRUSADE.

JACK: CAN THIS BE TRUE?

BLODWEN: JUST SEE WHAT I DO –
IT'S COMING THROUGH –
A PREZZY FOR YOU . . . !

(Fanfare. The Magic Sword descends from the flies ***(FlyQ.2; LXQ.13)*** *in a cloud of smoke and a blazing retrorocket.* ***(PyroQ.4)*** *Everybody can see this and they recoil in wonderment as JACK takes the sword and poses – heroic.)*

JACK:
JUST LOOK AT THAT!
A MAGIC SWORD –
TO HELP ME GAIN

THAT GREAT REWARD
WITH SWORD IN HAND,
I'LL FREE THE LAND
THEN FIX THE DATE
I MARRY KATE.

CHORUS:
JUST LOOK AT THAT
WHERE DID IT COME FROM?
SOMEONE MUST HAVE THROWN IT TO HIM
BUT WHO WAS IT?
HE'S PLAYING TRICKS ON US
WE ARE CERTAIN IT IS SO
STILL WE DON'T KNOW WHO DID IT
AND IT LOOKS LIKE WE MAY
NEVER KNOW!

(LXQ.14)

CHORUS: ALACK,
JUST LOOK AT THAT . . .
DEAR JACK,
WE WANT YOU BACK.
PERHAPS YOU NEED A REST
OR WOOLY VEST
OR ARE YOU OVERSTRESSED?
OR MAYBE YOU'RE KIDDING – DO YOU JEST?

BLODWEN: OFF YOU GO
TO FIGHT THE FOE
REMEMBER THOUGH
THE SWORD CAN ONLY BE DRAWN TO FIGHT A GIANT
AND NOBODY ELSE AT ALL.

JACK: I WON'T FORGET!

CHORUS: IT LOOKS AS THOUGH HE IS GETTING WORSE,

IT LOOKS AS THOUGH HE IS GETTING WORSE,
IT LOOKS AS THOUGH HE'S GETTING MUCH MUCH WORSE!

JACK:	CHORUS:
TO BE A HERO! A HERO!	TO SEE THE STATE THE LAD IS IN'S A NASTY SHOCK! ESPECIALLY AS HE'S NORM'LY STEADY AS A ROCK!
HERE'S MY CHANCE TO BE A HERO!	PERHAPS HE HAD A FALL AND GAVE HIS HEAD A KNOCK! SHOULD TRY TO KEEP HIM SAFE FROM HARM WITH KEY AND LOCK! A NASTY KNOCK! PLEASE DON'T MOCK! MUST TAKE STOCK!
ONWARD! TO VICTORY! ONWARD! TO VICTORY! TO VICTORY!	JUST SEE THE STATE THE LAD IS IN HAS HE BEEN KNOCKING BACK THE GIN? IS HE FEELING REALLY ILL AS TO HIMSELF HE'S TALKING STILL. POOR . . . POOR . . . JACK!

(BLODWEN flutters off DR.) ***(FSQ.7B; LXQ.15)*** *DAME LANSDOWN enters from the cottage, beating a mat.)*

DAME L: Do you mind? Do you flippin' mind? All this racket!

KATE: But, Dame Lansdown – I'm most awfully jolly worried about Jack.

DAME L: Shouldn't you be showjumping or something? Leave me to worry about Jack. Now be off with you . . . All of you . . . *(Smacking SIMON with the carpet beater.)* Not you!

(The VILLAGERS exit sadly to R and L.)

KATE: *(going DR)* I hope you're better soon, Jack . . .

JACK: Oh, Mother . . .

DAME L: What did she mean? What's up with you now?

JACK: The most wonderful thing just happened. I saw a fairy.

DAME L: Well, blow dry me bloomers, he's bats in the belfry!

JACK: But I did. Didn't I, friends?

AUDIENCE: YES.

DAME L: *(to AUDIENCE)* Oh you've been at the sherry trifle as well, have you?

JACK: And she told me that I will be a hero. That I'll slay the giant and avenge my father and marry Kate and be famous and the greatest hero that ever . . .

DAME L: Hero? Hero? I don't want to hear no more about heroes. Your poor father – *(Briefly emotional.)* lovely Long Larry – he was a hero and look what happened to him.

JACK: But look . . . The fairy gave me this sword . . .

DAME L: Fairy indeed! You've been spending your pocket money at Toys 'R' Us is what it is! Look: "Batteries not included". Now go and feed the chickens. Simon and me've got our hands full as it is.

JACK: Alright, Mother . . .

(JACK exits sadly DR.)

DAME L: *(taking SIMON into the cottage)* Now come on, Simon, I'll tell you what we have to do . . . I want a word with you about *(Tearfully.)* Daisy . . . !

(SIMON looks bewildered but sobs anyway. They exit into the Cottage. SIR BEASTLY enters furtively DL, carrying a large compass, a spade and a theodolite. He has the bag of beans and a dibber hanging from his belt.)

SIR BEASTLY: Secret and sneaky and skulking and sly
Slimy Sir Beastly slinks stealthily by.
I said I'd plant – 'em and I'm no fibber –
Here's me beans – and me little dibber.
I'll find the spot – the spot that's right –
By dangling my theodolite! *(He paces across to DR.)*

DAME L: *(re-enters from the cottage to LC)* It's Alan Titchmarsh and the Groundforce Team. I could lend Charlie my bra.

SIR BEASTLY: Just checking your property for the Council Tax, Madam. We think you're in the wrong band.

DAME L: I used to be with the Grateful Dead.

SIR BEASTLY: And were they?

DAME L: Not particularly.

(There is a great roar from BLUNDERBORE.) ***(SQ.11)***

SIR BEASTLY: *(calls upwards)* Coming!

(SIR BEASTLY paces carefully US to the front of the Cottage, squints through his theodolite, shuffles a few paces to C and checks his compass.)

SIR BEASTLY: *(aside)* If me co-ordinates is correct this must be directly beneath Blunderbore's portcullis. The very spot to plant me beans.

(He unslings his spade and starts to dig up the Dame's garden.)

DAME L: Just a minute, just a minute, just a minute! Do you mind? This is my front garden. It's private property. You can't go round digging things up like that. Who d'you think you are? Powergen?

SIR BEASTLY: *(strides DR – aside)* Curses. I must buy the old biddy's cooperation. *(Aloud, to R of DAME.)* A lovely house you have here, my good woman. I haven't had the pleasure.

DAME L: And you're not going to.

SIR BEASTLY: A charming Des Res. Gadzooks, and the air off of the industrial estate tastes like wine. What will you take for it?

DAME L: Take for it?

SIR BEASTLY: I'd like to buy it. Come now, money's no object.

DAME L: No. No, it's very tempting but this was my late husband's house. It's not much but it's home.

SIR BEASTLY: But my mind's made up.

DAME L: You wouldn't want this house.

SIR BEASTLY: Why not? Is it damp?

DAME L: Damp? We catch fish in the mousetraps.

SIR BEASTLY: Does it have running water?

DAME L: Every time it rains.

SIR BEASTLY: But it seems to be strong and stout.

DAME L: Strong and stout? The walls are so thin, whenever I peel onions, the people next door cry.

SIR BEASTLY: But enough of this. Just you listen to me, you old fleabag, I . . . *(He looks into her face for the first time. There is a DING! in the orchestra pit as he falls in love.)* Ah! *(Clutching his breast and staggering DL.)* You . . . Nay . . .

(Music: swirling Mantovani strings – "Charmaine" or similar.)

SIR BEASTLY: *(aside)* Be still my beating heart! Can this be . . . love? – that batters beneath me breastplate? Can such a nasty old ne'er do well as I be smitten? And by such a hideous old harridan? I know they say that love is blind but this is ridiculous. Yet how lovely she seems to me . . . That leathery skin . . .

DAME L: *(coy)* I use lemon juice for my complexion . . .

SIR BEASTLY: No wonder you look so sour . . . That rag-bag figure . . .

DAME L: I'm as fit as a fiddle.

SIR BEASTLY: But you look like a double bass. And that many wrinkles on her forehead she could screw her hat on. Yet she's the damsel I've dreamt of all these years . . . *(Approaching – oily.)* Dear lady . . . you may be a bat-eared, bogeyed biliously baleful and blotchy old biddy . . .

DAME L: I'm not *that* blotchy . . .

SIR BEASTLY: But, gadzooks, I love ye . . .

DAME L: Sir, I'm too young. I'm only twenty-eight.

SIR BEASTLY: I know. I counted the rings under your eyes. Oh, marry me and make me such a happy knight.

DAME L: I wouldn't marry you if it was crazy night.

SIR BEASTLY: I could improve. I could grow my hair.

DAME L: Over your face'd be a good idea.

SIR BEASTLY: You'd do well not to reject me. I'm a very nasty knight when crossed. You'll wish you'd said yes when I'm the King of Charlton Kings.

DAME L: King of Charlton Kings? You couldn't be Lord of Little Herberts!

SIR BEASTLY: Ah. You mock me. Not content to break my heart you twist the knife as well. Well! *(Tragic.) So* be it! For now, take my curse, foul, faithless filly! *(Aside, tearfully to the AUDIENCE.)* Me plan is thwarted. I shall return to me room to ruminate on rottenness . . . and the ravages of rejected romance!

(He sobs, broken hearted, and exits DL.)

DAME L: Ah love! Love is like a little green lizard – It runs up your leg and makes you feel wizard. But . . . Oh dear, did I do the right thing? Perhaps I *should* have sold him the house. We need the money, after all, to pay the Council Tax, the TV Tax, the Road Tax, the Value Added Tax, the Tin Tax . . . Not to mention the Cow Tax . . .

SIMON: *(enters from the Cottage to RC)* The Cow Tax?

DAME L: I said not to mention that. But then where would we live? No. There's only one thing for it. We'll have to sell . . . Daisy!

(Music: Dramatic Chord.)

SIMON: Sell . . . Daisy?!?

(Dramatic Chord.)

SIMON: Oh no!

(DAISY sticks her head out through the Cottage door.)

DAISY: MOOO?

DAME L: *(emotionally)* It's no use. She'll have to go. We must get her ready for . . . Gloucester market.

SIMON: Come on, Daisy. Out you come.

DAISY: *(shoves him away to R with her horns)* MOOO!

DAME L: Oooh! Daisy! You're a . . . NAUGHTY-NAUGHTY-COW!

DAISY: MOO!

DAME L: We'll have to coax her out.

SIMON: But how do we do that, Dame Lansdown?

DAME L: Watch this. *(Sings.)* Oh Arthur, Oh Arthur, don't be so unkind. Please don't stick your pitchfork up Daisy's behind.

(DAISY reacts violently, and trots swiftly out of the Cottage to DC.)

DAME L: Isn't she a love, boys and girls? I'll just give you a guided tour. Now you see, Daisy's got two sticker-uppers, four hanger downers and a swisher.

(DAISY swishes her tail and knocks SIMON over.)

DAME L: You're a . . . NAUGHTY-NAUGHTY-COW!

DAISY: MOOOO!

DAME L: Actually, I bought her from an Arab dairy farmer.

SIMON: An Arab dairy farmer?

DAME L: He was a milk sheik. Now pay attention. Before we can clean her, we have to milk her.

(DAISY folds up.)

DAME L: Daisy! You . . . What is she, boys and girls? She's a . . . *(Leading the AUDIENCE.)* NAUGHTY-NAUGHTY-COW! Right. Now, Simon, I hope you can manage it this time. The last time you tried to milk her, it was udder chaos.

SIMON: Remind me how to do it, Dame Lansdown.

DAME L: You just go round the back and pump the tail.

(They both walk round to R and DAISY rotates with them.)

DAME L: No no. Round the back, you simple Simon.

(They circle round to L and, again, DAISY rotates with them. SIMON turns to milk her and jumps when he finds he's at the wrong end.)

DAME L: Simon!

(Simon has an idea – "DING!" He ducks down and crawls underneath DAISY from front to tail.)

DAME L: Ooo, I wouldn't go under there, dear. You might get a pat on the head. Now – pumping stations!

(SIMON crawls out hurriedly and begins to pump DAISY'S tail up and down. A bottle of milk drops out of the udder.)

SIMON: *(picking it up)* Oh look – semi-skilled.

DAME L: Keep pumping.

(SIMON throws the milk bottle offstage R – SWANEE WHISTLE – and pumps again. A purple tin tray drops out with a crash.)

SIMON: *(picking it* up) What's that, Dame Lansdown?

DAME L: That's the Cadbury's milk tray.

SIMON: *(throws the tray off and bends to inspect DAISY'S udder)* What are all these bits here for, Dame Durdham?

DAME L: Those are the working bits, dear. *(Pointing to each in turn.)* See, this one's four star. This one's unleaded.

This one's diesel. And this one's . . . *(She squirts the practical udder into SIMON'S face.)* . . . The udder one.

SIMON: *(pumping – sings)* "When I fall in love, it will be for heifer . . .

(A bottle of milk stout drops out.)

SIMON: Oh look. *(Picking it up.)* Milk stout. This'll put hairs on your chest, Dame Lansdown.

DAME L: I don't need things like that.

(SIMON throws the bottle off – SWANEE WHISTLE.)

DAME L: My skin is beautiful. Why? Because I bathe in milk.

SIMON: Pasteurised?

DAME L: No. Only up to here. But it's wonderful for me wrinkles.

SIMON: *(to AUDIENCE)* She doesn't have wrinkles. She has pleats.

DAME L: I heard that, Simon. Now. Go and get – *(Dramatic.)* – the Tesco trolley.

SIMON: *(aghast)* The Tesco trolley?

DAME L: The Tesco trolley . . .

SIMON: If you're really sure . . . *(He exits L.)*

DAME L: *(puts her hand on DAISY'S forehead)* You're very hot dear? You got a temperature? Better give you some Cowpol . . .

(SIMON returns pushing a supermarket trolley containing a milking stool, a metal bucket, a huge Powder Puff, Scent Spray, Cotton buds, Loofah and a long-handled backscrubber.)

DAME L: Now, Daisy, you're going to like this . . .

SIMON: Not a lot.

(DAME LANSDOWN places the milking stool behind DAISY and turns away to get the bucket. DAISY kicks the stool over.)

DAME L: You . . . NAUGHTY-NAUGHTY-COW! Smacky botty.

(She replaces the stool. SIMON bends to pick up the bucket. DAISY kicks the bucket over with her back foot and butts SIMON with her horns, causing him to get his head stuck in the bucket. He wanders about blindly, hands outstretched.)

DAME L: Well! You really are a . . . NAUGHTY-NAUGHTY-COW!

(SIMON is about to plunge into the orchestra pit.)

DAME L: Simon! Pull yourself together.

(She takes the stool and replaces it. DAISY kicks it over again and butts SIMON so that, this time, he steps into the bucket and gets his foot stuck.)

DAME L: This is getting us nowhere!

SIMON: I'll polish the horns. *(He goes to the horns with a duster. He rings the bicycle bell.)* Why has she got a bell, Dame Lansdown?

DAME L: 'Cos that horn doesn't work, dear. Right. Now we give her a brush – and you, Simon, clean her ears with the cotton bud . . .

(DAISY giggles and moos and wriggles.)

DAME L: Oh, pull yourself together, Daisy dear. Now for the scent *(She takes a huge scent spray.)* It's udder cologne . . . *(She sprays the udder. DAISY moos in ecstasy.)* Right, dear, get the powder puff and give her a dusting . . .

(SIMON takes a huge powder puff and dabs clouds of powder onto DAISY. DAISY gives a massive sneeze and SIMON and DAME LANSDOWN fall over. They get up. DAISY sneezes again and they both fall over again. They get up. DAISY starts to build for another sneeze but SIMON puts a finger under her nose and it stops her. Relieved, DAME LANSDOWN goes to put the scent spray back in the trolley.)

DAME L: Now then . . .

(She is bending over it when DAISY lets go with the biggest sneeze yet. SIMON falls into DAME LANSDOWN who shoots offstage L on the trolley. There is a crash. DAME LANSDOWN staggers back on.)

DAME L: Really, Daisy, you're a . . . *(Becoming suddenly emotional.)* Oh dear. You look lovely dear. And I shall miss you so. Because . . .

(LXQ.16; FSQ.8)

Song: DAISY BELL *(DAME, SIMON, JACK and KATE)*

DAME L: THERE IS A FLOWER WITHIN MY HEART,

BOTH: DAISY! DAISY!

(JACK and KATE enter R.)

SIMON: A COW LIKE NO UDDER RIGHT FROM THE START –

BOTH: NO UDDER LIKE DAISY BELL.

(FSQ.8A)

JACK: OH, MOTHER, OH, MOTHER WHY MUST SHE GO?

KATE: SHE'S PART OF THE FAMILY

DAME L: I PROMISE, AS SOON AS I'VE GOT THE DOUGH
I'LL BUY HER BACK INSTANTLY.
BUT:

JACK: BUT . . .

SIMON: BUT . . .

KATE: *(completing the chord)* BUT . . .

DAISY: *(ruining the chord)* MOOOOOO!

(As they sing the chorus, DAME LANSDOWN and SIMON lead DAISY across to R in front of the cottage. JACK and KATE follow to be L of DAISY.)

ALL: DAISY, DAISY, WE HAVE TO PART WITH YOU.

IT MAY SEEM CRAZY BUT THE TAXES ARE
OVERDUE.
WE CAN'T AFFORD TO FEED YOU –

SO, EVEN THOUGH WE NEED YOU,
IT'S NOW . . . "GOODBYE" . . .
BUT PLEASE . . . DON'T CRY . . .
WE WILL ALWAYS REMEMBER YOU.

(LXQ.17; FSQ.8B)

(By which time, they are all sobbing helplessly and the music continues sadly during:)

DAISY: *(miserably)* MOOO!

DAME L: It's no use. I can't bear it. You'll have to take her to market, Jack . . .

JACK: But, Mother . . .

DAME L: *(very dramatic)* You'll have to! You'll have to! I can't do it, d'you understand? But be sure and get a good price for her. Never let it be said that we parted with our pet for peanuts. Goodbye, Daisy . . .

SIMON: *(sobbing)* Goodbye, Daisy . . .

JACK: But, Mother . . .

KATE: Oh, Jack, I know it's hard. But I'll come with you part of the way . . . Come on, Daisy . . .

JACK: But, mother, she's like one of the family.

DAME L: On your father's side. Now come on – steel yourself. You must take her from here to somewhere over there and see what you can get for her and don't come back until, you've . . . sold her.

DAISY: MOOOOOOOOO!

DAME L: *(weeping)* Goodbye, Daisy. Be a good girl now. Whoever buys you, I want you to show them what a well-brought-up little cow you are. *(She blows her nose at great length and then rings her hanky out into the bucket – which SIMON holds.)* Goodbye . . .

DAISY: MOOO!

SIMON: *(weeping)* Goodbye, Daisy. You lovely old moo.

JACK: Alright. There's no other way, Daisy. Come on . . .

(Sad journey music – DAISY BELL. As JACK and KATE lead DAISY from R to L (mime-walk), DAME LANSDOWN and SIMON shuffle sideways to R, still waving and weeping, at the same pace as the Cottage and the hedgerows – creating a horizontal "journey" transformation. Just as DAME LANSDOWN and SIMON are vanishing into the wings, JACK suddenly can't do it. JACK, DAISY and KATE run back to R and the Cottage, DAME LANSDOWN and SIMON return at speed.)

JACK: Oh, Mother. Surely we could . . .

DAME L: No! Now go. Please, please GO!!

SIMON: *(keening – hugely dramatic)* Oh no . . . Oh . . . Woe! No! No! NO!!

DAME L: For pity's sake . . . *(To stop him over-acting.)* GO!!

DAISY: MOO-OO-OOOOO!

(They set off again and, this time, the change is completed when the Cottage, SIMON and DAME LANSDOWN are offstage R and the last piece of hedge is on from L with a sign saying "TO MARKET – NOT FAR".)

Scene Three

On the road to Market.

JACK: *(calling)* Cow for sale. Cow for sale.

DAISY: MOOO!

KATE: Oh we must cheer up. We can't let Daisy remember us like this. I don't want to leave Daisy so downhearted.

JACK: But, if only we weren't so poor. It's all the fault of Blunderbore.

Music *(Intro)*: SIDE BY SIDE *(JACK and KATE)*

(LXQ.18; FSQ.9)

KATE: We may be poor but we're together just for the moment. Let's enjoy being with Daisy while we can.

(Sings.) SEE THAT SUN IN THE MORNING –
LOOKING OVER THE HILL
SEEMS TO ME IT ALWAYS HAS
AND IT ALWAYS WILL . . .

JACK & KATE: THOUGH WE DON'T HAVE A BARREL OF MONEY
MAYBE WE'RE RAGGED AND FUNNY
BUT WE'LL TRAVEL ALONG,
SINGING A SONG,
SIDE BY SIDE.
DON'T KNOW WHAT'S COMING TOMORROW –
MAYBE IT'S TROUBLE AND SORROW –
BUT WE'LL TRAVEL THE ROAD –
SHARING OUR LOAD –
SIDE BY SIDE.
THROUGH ALL KINDS OF WEATHER,
WHAT IF THE SKY SHOULD FALL?
AS LONG AS WE'RE TOGETHER,
IT JUST DOESN'T MATTER AT ALL.
WHEN THEY'VE ALL HAD THEIR TROUBLES AND PARTED –
WE'LL BE THE SAME AS WE STARTED –
TRAVELLING ALONG
SINGING A SONG –
SIDE BY SIDE.

(LXQ.19; FSQ.9A)

KATE: Goodbye, Daisy . . .

(KATE exits R in tears.)

JACK: I hope I can find a really nice owner for you, Daisy. *(Calling.)* Cow for sale . . . Cow going cheap . . .

(SIR BEASTLY, disguised as a Gypsy, carrying a crystal ball (on elastic) and the bag of beans peeps round the proscenium.)

SIR BEASTLY: I thought cows went moo. *(Lurching on in "character" and making an awful attempt at a Brum accent.)*
Here cooms Gypsy Joe!
From the Black Coontry, don't yow know?
Oi'll tell you your fortune with a hey nonny no!
And wheetle soom clowspegs afore oi go.

JACK: Oh. Are you a gypsy?

SIR BEASTLY: You're queek, aren't you? But, oh dear, yoong ma-a-aster. Whoy so glum?

JACK: I have to sell our cow and we don't want to be parted.

SIR BEASTLY: But, surely, if she was gaween to a good 'ome.

JACK: That's what I'm hoping.

SIR BEASTLY: Oi could give her a very good 'ome and – boy the most amazing coincidence, Oi'm in need of a cow joost now. Oi've a coopboard full of Cocopops and not a drop of meelk.

JACK: What will you pay me? I have to get a good price or mother'll be furious.

SIR BEASTLY: A good proice? Mooney d'yow mean? Oi'll do better than that, lad. Oi'll give yow these . . . there now. *(Giving him the bag of beans.)* Did yow ever see the loike of them before?

JACK: But they're just . . . beans . . .

SIR BEASTLY: Joost beans? *(Snatching them back.)* Joost beans? These, moy lad, are mageec beans.

JACK: Mageec . . . ? I mean – magic beans? You're pulling my leg. I never heard of magic beans . . .

SIR BEASTLY: Then let me enloighten you, lad . . . *(Dropping the accent.)* Oh blow this for a game of soldiers . . . First, these beans don't just grow in the Summer. You'll have beans of all sorts the whole year through. I tell you, lad and you tell your Ma – these beans are a passport to permanent flatulence . . . and they don't just grow beans neither . . .

JACK: They don't?

SIRBEASTLY: Why no. Not magic beans. Magic beans'll grow whatever your heart desires . . . Pods of fudge and sugar candy.
Pods of banknotes – they come in handy.
Pods of plenty for young and old . . .
Pods of pearls and pods of gold,

JACK: Gold?

SIRBEASTLY: Gold, diamonds, wealth beyond your wildest dreams.

JACK: It seems like a good deal.

SIRBEASTLY: You'll never getta a better.

JACK: I have to be careful, you see, 'cos Mum thinks I'm a bit thick.

SIRBEASTLY: I wonder what gave her that idea . . .

JACK: I'll take it.

SIRBEASTLY: You'll never regret it.

JACK: You don't sound like a Gypsy anymore.

SIRBEASTLY: *(resuming the accent)* Oi've a norful cold. Boot . . . !

JACK: Boot?

SIRBEASTLY: Yow moost be careful to plant 'em een your froont gardeeng – joost three feet south of the froont doower.

JACK: Three feet south?

SIRBEASTLY: Of the froont doower. And now. Farewell, me doock. *(Aside to the AUDIENCE.)* Success! It worked! I told you you'd see – tomorrow, Cheltenham belongs to me! *(In his excitement, he drops the crystal ball on his foot.)* AHHHH!!! Oh . . . Coom on, cow, walk thees way . . .

(He limps grotesquely off DL followed by DAISY, copying his walk. She gives one last sad "MOOO" before disappearing.)

JACK: Goodbye, Daisy . . . Oh, Daisy, I . . . But magic beans. Mother'll be so happy. She can't say I'm a fool and a dreamer after I give her these. Magic beans! And, if I run, I might still be in time to meet Kate at the Squire's birthday party . . .

(Blackout.) ***(LXQ.20)***

(FlyQ.3)

Scene Four

A Clearing in the Forest. ***(LXQ.21)***

(FSQ.10)

SIMON enters playing "Happy Birthday to You" on his trumpet (or whatever instrument) and leading the VILLAGERS playing Kazoos or whatever they can play. Two of them are pushing a wheelbarrow loaded with instruments – Tuba, Trombone, Tenor Horn, etc.

(LXQ.22; FSQ.10A)

SIMON: Three cheers for Squire Freddy the Unsteady. Hip hip!

(Fanfare.)

ALL: CHEER.

(SIR BEASTLY enters, carrying a large pair of cymbals, limping as before, with his foot bound up a huge gout bandage. The cheers change to boos and hisses.)

SIR BEASTLY: *(snarling)* Alright! Alright! I don't like you either!

(The SQUIRE peeps round the proscenium L, waving to SIMON.)

SIMON: Three cheers for Squire Freddy the Unsteady who is now ready. Hip hip . . .

(Fanfare. Cheers. The SQUIRE enters flamboyantly, trips as he reaches C, rolls over a couple of times and lands on his feet.)

SQUIRE: My dear peasants, unaccustomed as I am to public speaking, I have prepared a short address . . .

ALL: GROAN.

SIMON: Why is he wearing a shorter dress?

SQUIRE: Though times are hard, though we live in constant terror of the giant Blunderbore, yet I know that I can count on your loyalty and high regard . . .

(DAME LANSDOWN enters from DR, wearing and beating a bass marching drum.)

DAME L: *(with the AUDIENCE)* Oggy, oggy, oggy . . . *(Etc.)*

SQUIRE: Dame Lansdown? What's all this?

DAME L: It's the Fiddlers Green Silver Band, Squire.

SQUIRE: Band . . . ?

DAME L: Banned from everywhere else You remember the band that made a cacophony at the Gold Cup?

SQUIRE: Only too well.

DAME L: Well we've come to do a boom-boom on your birthday.

SQUIRE: But I didn't know you were musicians?

DAME L: It all started at Christmas, your Squireship. I was given a trombone and a bottle of perfume.

SQUIRE: A trombone and a bottle of perfume?

DAME L: Yes. So, if you hear a little noise and smell a little smell – it's me. Now. Get your instruments, everybody. We've been practicing, to show how much we admire our Squire.

SQUIRE: When I was born, you know, they fired a twenty-one gun salute.

SIR BEASTLY: Pity they missed.

SQUIRE: But surely I don't have to just listen. Can't I join in?

DAME L: Can you play the piano by ear?

SQUIRE: No but I can fiddle with my whiskers.

DAME L: Well, you can either have a tinkle on the triangle or tootle on the tuba.

SQUIRE: I've just had a tinkle.

DAME L: *(handing him the tuba)* In that case, you'd better tootle. *(To everybody.)* Now have you all got your instruments?

ALL: Yes, Dame Lansdown . . .

DAME L: Right. The first thing is to tune up. I'll give you an A.

(She beats the drum as everybody else blows the loudest and most dischordant sound.)

SIMON: Stop! Stop! That was terrible. Your flutes are a hoot, your piccolos are pitiful, your kazoos are chronic and your cymbals are a shambles! Try again!

DAME L: I'll give you an A.

(Again the same terrible noise to begin with but gradually coalescing onto a beautiful chord.)

SIMON: Perfect! Now, after three . . . Three!

(They all launch into a loud approximation of "POET AND PEASANT". DAME LANSDOWN is hypnotised by SIR BEASTLY'S gout foot and tries to hit it on the "boom booms" but, as he crashes his cymbals, so his foot twitches out of the way – until the last chance when she gets him. SIR BEASTLY screams with pain and fury then crashes his cymbals in her face, leaving her wobbling.)

SIMON: And now . . . a three, four – a one, two, three, four!

(They launch into "WHEN THE SAINTS GO MARCHING IN", marching round the stage to exit L.)

(LXQ.23; SQ.14)

(Music: ROMANTIC PASTORAL. The lights fade to a beautiful sunset as FAIRY BLODWEN flutters on gracefully.)

BLODWEN: The sun sinks over Springbank
Bathing Arle in a golden hue.

*(Night falls suddenly – **(LXQ.24)** – with an accompanying "thud" from the pit.)*

BLODWEN: There's a twilight shade over Regent Arcade
And it's bed-time at GCHQ.
Battledown's benighted –
Robins have lost – eight-nil –
And there's nary a sound
Throughout the town –
Save for the giggles on Warden Hill.

(SQ.15) *(SIR BEASTLY creeps on DL.)*

SIR BEASTLY: Private and privy I pass me portcullis –
Silent I sneak to see no one's in sight –
Crafty I crawl round behind the Town Hall –
I see it's a villain's moon tonight!

BLODWEN: Hold!

SIR BEASTLY: Hold what?

BLODWEN: There's late you are to be loiterin' innit?

SIR BEASTLY: I'm not loitering in it, you Welsh witch. I'm about my business.

BLODWEN: Beastly business, I'll be bound.

SIR BEASTLY: Not at all. Why must you always think the worst of me? I've . . . I've lost me little pussy and it's time for her bedtime milk. *(Calling.)* Pilchard? Pilchard . . . *(He exits DL.)* Where's my little Pilchard . . . ?

(Off L, a cat miaows and spits. ***(SQ.16)*** *There is a scream of pain from SIR BEASTLY.)*

BLODWEN: He's up to something, that much I knows –
Best keep an eye and stay on me toes.
I'll find out what Sir Beastly's got planned.
But here come the lovers – hand in hand . . . There's lovely . . . *(Going.)* Sssshhh . . .

(She flutters off DR as JACK and KATE enter from L.)

(FSQ.11)

Song: WHY DON'T MY DREAMS COME TRUE? *(JACK and KATE)*

JACK/KATE: MY LIFE IS FILLED WITH DREAMS,
WITH VISIONS RICH AND RARE,
A DREAMBOY/GIRL RULES MY HEART,
I SEEK HER/HIM EV'RYWHERE –

ALL OF THE DAY I AM DREAMING,
AND IN THE NIGHT TIME, TOO.
SEEKING THE FACE THAT I DREAM OF,
SEEMS NO ONE ELSE WILL DO.
OFF – IN A CLOUD I GO SAILING,
SEARCHING THE WHOLE WORLD THROUGH.
BUT THERE'S NO END TO MY RAINBOW
WHY DON'T MY DREAMS COME TRUE?

(Blackout.) ***(LXQ.25; FSQ.11A)***

(FlyQ.4; LXQ.26)

Scene Five

Inside DAME LANSDOWN'S Cottage.

Door URC, Window UC, high bunk beds running up and down stage either side with ladders at the downstage end for access. A wardrobe UL is actually DAME LANSDOWN'S bed which folds down. There is a big old-fashioned radio on a shelf below the bunk R. A rustic chandelier hangs C.

DAME LANSDOWN is seen passing the window, beating her drum feebly. She enters and totters DC, falling forward onto her drum and almost rolling right over it.

DAME L: *(slipping her shoulders out of the straps)* Oh isn't it a relief to get the straps off, girls? *(She puts the drum out of the way UR.)* There now.

(She picks up a large remote control zapper, points it at the chandelier and clicks. The light comes on. ***(LXQ.27)*** *She points it at the window and clicks – the curtains close. Click – they open. Click – they close. She opens and shuts them faster and faster then, leaving them open, she points at the radio and clicks.* ***(SQ.17 – Disco Music.)*** *She dances across towards the wardrobe, click – the doors fly open and her bed comes down with a crash. She points at the bed, click – a chamber pot shoots out.)*

DAME L: Not you! Not yet! *(She clicks and it disappears under the bed. She exits DL, calling:)* Jack! Where are you?

JACK: *(entering URC – with the bag of beans)* Here Mother. *(Excited.)* Mother, you'll never guess what happened. I met this gypsy and . . .

(Music: A PRETTY GIRL. DAME LANSDOWN sidles on from DL in very Barbara Cartland sort of nightwear.)

DAME L: Oh, Jack, lad. D'you know, sometimes I feel like I did when I was twenty-one. Isn't that amazing?

JACK: As a feat of memory, yes!

DAME L: I feel I'm on the brink of something exciting. You know that Sir B? He fancies me!

JACK: You've got to be joking.

DAME L: But enough of my beauty and ravishingness Tell me about Daisy? *(Tearfully.)* Did you manage to . . . sell her?

JACK: That's what I was trying to tell you. I met this gypsy who gave me these . . .

DAME L: *(ecstatic)* Oh Jack! Money at last. The end of all our troubles. Now we won't be thrown out. Now I can do the midweek Lottery.

JACK: There are better things than money, Mother . . .

DAME L: Of course there are, dear . . . I just can't quite remember what they are. Now come on – give us the lolly.

JACK: *(giving her the bag)* Here you are, Mother, but . . .

DAME L: *(weighing the bag in her hands)* It's heavy. Weighs a ton. There must be fifty gold coins in here. Maybe a hundred.

JACK: Better than that. But, Mother . . .

DAME L: Better? Oh, Jack, you clever lad. I'll never be angry with you again . . . Now let's see . . . *(Opening the bag.)* I'll never call you thick or stupid or gormless or . . . What's this? *(Taking out a handful.)* Beans? Beans? You thick . . . You stupid . . . You gormless . . . You sold Daisy for a bag of beans? They're no use. What can I do with beans? What are beans fit for? *(To the AUDIENCE.)* What's that? Throw them out of the window? And that's what I'm going to do. Shall I throw them out, boys and girls?

AUDIENCE: Yes.

DAME L: Shall I?

AUDIENCE: YES!

DAME L: *(putting them down on her bed)* But first – I must get ready for bed. And as for you you big Wodjuk . . . Get ready for bed. *(Calling.)* Simon! Simon? Where are you?

SIMON: *(entering URC)* It can't go on. It can't go on. It can *not* go on.

DAME L: What can't?

SIMON: *(producing a tiny pyjama top)* My jammy top. It's shrunk.

DAME L: You stupid boy, Now get ready for bed. Clean your teeth. Come on, we need our beauty sleep.

JACK: Does sleep make you beautiful?

DAME L: Yes.

SIMON: Well you must've been awake a lot.

DAME L: Shut up and come and clean your teeth. I'll get the stuff. *(She goes off DL.)*

JACK: My Mum's got teeth like stars.

SIMON: Has she?

JACK: Yeah. They come out at night.

(DAME LANSDOWN returns with a large toothbrush, a glass of water and a bucket. She gives the brush to JACK, the glass to SIMON and holds the bucket in front of herself.)

JACK: Right. Ready?

SIMON: Ready.

(JACK brushes his teeth, SIMON drinks the water. DAME LANSDOWN gargles and spits into the bucket. CHORD from the pit. They bow.)

DAME L: Now go to bed. Go on! Straight into bed and your light out. No reading and leave your Playstation alone – you know what happened last time you played with your joystick. Beans indeed!

(SIMON goes to collect and cuddle Bunny.)

JACK: *(climbing into the top bunk R)* But, Mother . . . they're magic beans . . .

DAME L: Magic? I'll magic you! Whoever heard of magic beans? Now go to sleep!

JACK: *(sadly)* Yes, Mother. But Mother . . .

DAME L: Not another word.

SIMON: *(climbing into the top bunk L)* Oh alright, Dame Letitia. *(Holds out fluffy Bunny.)* Kiss my bunny.

DAME L: Good night, little bunny. *(She punches it.)*

BUNNY: OOH!

SIMON: *(tearfully)* She bashed my bunny!

DAME L: Now go to sleep. Say good night, Jack and Simon.

BOTH: *(giggling)* Good night Jack and Simon.

DAME L: Good night! Now have I done everything? I've locked the cat, put out the door and shut the milk bottle. Now is there anything else I should chuck out?

AUDIENCE: BEANS.

DAME L: Oh yes. The beans. D'you mean these beans?

AUDIENCE: Yes.

DAME L: Honestly! Whoever heard of magic beans? Shall I chuck them out of the window?

AUDIENCE: Yes.

DAME L: Alright. You know best. Are you sure?

AUDIENCE: YES!

DAME L: ONE . . . TWO . . . THREE . . . *(She throws the beans out of the window.)* And good riddance.

(As she turns away, there is a clap of Thunder.) ***(SQ.18)***

DAME L: Looks like rain. That'll make a change. *(Climbing into bed.)* Oh well . . . Nightie nightie.

SIMON/JACK: Pyjama pyjama . . .

(She zaps the lights out. ***(LXQ.28)*** *They all snuggle down, grunting, snorting and snoring, to sleep. Music.* ***(LXQ.29)*** *Through the window, we see the beanstalk begin to grow.* ***(FlyQ.5)*** *There is a creaking and rending* ***(SQ.19)*** *as it apparently begins to split the cottage in two.* ***(LXQ.30)*** *Great cracks appear in the wall and ceiling C* ***(SQ.20)*** *and the trucks move off to R and L as the scene transforms to:)*

Scene Six

DAME LANSDOWN'S Garden.

The beanstalk continues to grow upwards as the Chorus of Beans dance on ***(LXQ.31)*** *for the BEAN BALLET. At a point during this,* ***(FSQ.12)*** *DAME LANSDOWN pirouttes across from L to R among the dancers wearing a Heinz Baked Beans tin.*

(FSQ.12A)

As the ballet ends, ***(LXQ.32)*** *the beanstalk is fully grown and JACK enters from UR, rubbing the sleep from his eyes.*

JACK: What's happening? What is it? *(Calling.)* Mother!

DAME L: *(enters from UR, sleepwalking)* No! No, I won't go out with Richard Whitely. I will not go out with Richard Whitely . . .

JACK: Mother, wake up!

DAME L: I am awake. I will not go out with Richard Whitely . . . What's happening? *(She turns and sees the beanstalk.)* Aaaahhh! Get on to Gardeners' Question Time straight away . . .

(SIMON, SQUIRE, KATE and the VILLAGERS rush on from R and L.)

KATE: What's happening? Jack?

SQUIRE: What is it? What's up?

JACK: The beans, look! The magic beans . . . They've grown a beanstalk right up into the clouds . . . Right up to the giant's castle!

(SQ.21)

SIMON: But that's terrible! Don't you realise? Old Blunderbore'll come down and terrorise the town!

(All scream in terror.)

SQUIRE: Just like he did before Long Larry Lansdown broke down the stone stairs . . .

(All scream in terror.)

DAME L: We'll be Blunderbore's brunch . . .

(All scream in terror.)

JACK: Don't be afraid, Mother. I'll climb up there and fight him.

DAME L: You? Fight the giant? Don't be so silly . . .

*(Everybody laughs scornfully at JACK and they turn away US to the beanstalk. A Flash. **(PyroQ.5; LXQ.33; FSQ.13)** FAIRY BLODWEN appears DR.)*

BLODWEN: Fear nothing, Jack, for this is your chance to win glory and acclaim.

You'll fight the fight
For truth and right
And save all here from fear and shame.
If you but hold
To your dream so bold,

You'll triumph over all –
And then no more
Shall Blunderbore
Hold Cheltenham in his thrall.

JACK: I'll do it. I will! I'll do it!

ALL: *(moving down in a line to address the AUDIENCE)* Who's he talking to?

AUDIENCE: The fairy!

ALL: The fairy?

(FSQ.13A)

Finale: The Miserere from *'Il Trovatore* *(ALL)*

ALL: OH, JACK, ARE YOU RAVING?
SO DAFT YOU'RE BEHAVING –
YOU'VE JUST STARTED SHAVING –
YOU'RE TOO YOUNG TO DIE!

KATE: UP THERE, WHERE THE BEANSTALK FLOW'RS –

SIMON: AND BLUNDERBORE TOWERS
IN HIS POWERS

KATE: AND HE GLOWERS

DAME D: AND DEVOURS YOU FOR LUNCH!

KATE: AH, JACK!
I, JACK,
HAVE A
HUNCH, JACK,
YOU'RE A
LUNCHPACK;
SO, JACK,
IT'S GOODBY-Y-Y-YE-E-E!

(LXQ.34)

JACK:	ALL:
HARK, I HEAR GLORY CALL ME –	
	WOE . . .
ECHOING HIGH ABOVE –	
	WOE . . .
SPURNING ALL DOUBT –	

WOE . . .

SIR B: BLIND FOOLS!

FEARLESS, I'LL CLIMB THE SPROUT
TO KILL AND QUELL –
PEOPLE OF CHELTENHAM,
FAREWELL!

WOE AND ALACK! SIR BEASTLY RULES NOW!
OH POOR, POOR JACK!
IS HE PAST SAVING?

SIMON, KATE, VILLAGERS:
(at the beanstalk) IT'S TREMENDOUS!
IT'S REALLY QUITE STUPENDOUS!
HOW COULD IT GROW SO BIG WITHOUT SUSPENDERS?
WHO'D HAVE THOUGHT IT?
BEANS ARE USUALLY SHORT, IT'S
DAME LANSDOWN'S BEANSTALK –
WONDER WHERE SHE BOUGHT IT?

JACK:
NOW DESTINY'S BECKONING!
A DREAMER I'LL BE NO MORE.
IT'S TIME FOR THE RECKONING
WITH VILE BLUNDERBORE!

SIMON/VILLAGERS:
OH, BY GOLLY!
WHAT A WALLY!

HE IS AFTER –

GETTING DAFTER –

KATE:
FAREWELL THEN, MY HERO.

'SCUSE OUR LAUGHTER

DAME D:
JUST MIND HOW YOU GO.

SIMON: WE WILL WAIT HERE BELOW
WHILE YOU VANQUISH THE FOE . . .

KATE: OH, JACK!

VILLAGERS: WE'RE . . .

SIMON: NO, JACK!

ALRI-I-I-I . . .

DAME D: PLEASE DON'T
GO JACK.

I-I-IGHT . . .
JACK!

SIMON: COME BACK!

DAME D: UNPACK!

ALL: ALACK! OH . . .

(LXQ.35)

WOE, THIS COULD BE DISASTER!
THE WHOLE PLOT BEGINS TO SMELL.
WOE! OH! ALACK!
WHEN WILL OUR JACK COME BACK?
OH FARE THEE WELL!
HE'S UP THE BEANSHOOT,
FAREWELL!

KATE: I QUAKE!
MY HEART WILL BREAK!
SEE HOW I SHAKE!

BLODWEN:
BRAVE LAD, WE THANK YE!

VILLAGERS:
MAKES US SICK, SO –

SIR B: EGAD!

DAME D:
OH, DEAR ME!

THE LAD IS MAD!

VILLAGERS:
ON OUR WICK-O

BLODWEN: YOU'RE SUCH A CAD!

SIMON:
HERE, USE MY HANKY.

SIR B:
YOU'D BEST BELIEVE IT.

DAME D: OH, MY POOR BOY –

VILLAGERS:
WHO'D HAVE THOUGHT
HE'D BE A THICKO?

SIR B: HE WON'T ACHIEVE IT!

DAME D: MY LITTLE PRIDE AND JOY!

BLODWEN: HE'LL BE A GALAHAD!

DAME D: OH, WHO WILL FEED HIS HAMSTER NOW?

BLODWEN:
HE'LL FIGHT

VILLAGERS:

FOR WHAT IS RIGHT
AND NEVER TAKE FRIGHT.

UP THE TREE, THOUGH –
HE'LL BE A HERO –

SIR B: HE'LL MAKE
A MINUTE STEAK
A GIANT'S LIGHT-BITE.

(LXQ.36)

ALL: BUT GIVE THE LAD
A HERO'S CHEER.

BLODWEN: COME, BEASTLY,
CHEER HIM!

HE'S GOING FAR FROM HERE.

SIR B: I'LL NOT GO NEAR HIM.

GIVE HIM A CHEER

VILLAGERS: AND SAVE US
FROM THE GIANT FOE.

AS HE CLIMBS WITHOUT FEAR

SIR B: I'M GOING FOR A BEER
AND A CORNETTO

RIGHT UP INTO THE STRATOSPHERE.

SIR B: SEE YOU – IN TWENTY
MINUTES – BACK HERE.

GIVE HIM A CHEER!

VILLAGERS: SO, FOR GLORY,
GIVE A CHEER!

(LXQ.37; FSQ.13B)

(Curtain. End of Act One.)

ACT TWO

(LXQ.38)

Scene One

Above the clouds.

Music: THE SABRE DANCE (RAVEN'S DANCE)

The top of the beanstalk grows up through a trap centre stage. Blunderbore's castle on the cloth, seen in the distance. Thick clouds among which Ravens are dancing. A crash of thunder, the Ravens squawk and fly off as SIR BEASTLY appears, climbing up the beanstalk (through the trap).

(LXQ.39; FSQ.14; SQ.22)

SIR BEASTLY: Wey hey and UP I rises –
Up the beanstalk – full of surprises –
No need now of cunning disguises –
Now to claim my major prizes . . .

(Flash. ***(PyroQ.6; LXQ.40, FSQ.15)*** *FAIRY BLODWEN appears DR.)*

BLODWEN: Not you again!
Dew, there's a Pain!
And how d'you get here first?

SIR BEASTLY: I nipped round the back
Of that stupid Jack
And now to do my worst!

BLODWEN: Not so fast! Hold on a minute!
If there's a fight, young Jack'll win it.
That Blunderboyo'll be beaten, innit?
You cheeky thing!

SIR BEASTLY: I've but to lead the Giant down
For him to terrorise the town
And then they'll beg me to take the crown
As Charlton's King!

BLODWEN: Now listen, bach – pin back your ears –
I've had my eye on you for years –
I'm proper sick of your nasty sneers
And your dirty look!

SIR BEASTLY: Don't call me "bach", you Fairy blight!
I'm nobody's "bach" I'm a noble knight.

BLODWEN: *(smugly)* You'll find my bach is worse than my bite!
'Less you sling your hook!
I've had it up to here with yewer
Dirty deeds and that's for su-ere.

SIR BEASTLY: I'm off to wake up BLUNDERBU-ERE!
Then you'll be in shtook!

(Clap of Thunder. ***(SQ.23; LXQ.41; FSQ.14A)*** *He exits DL, cackling nastily.)*

BLODWEN: *(to audience)* Don't worry, loves. For Jack's ascending
The beanstalk now – see how it's bending –
And on his courage we're all depending
To bring about a happy ending!

(She skips off joyfully. ***(FSQ.15A; LXQ.42)*** *JACK climbs out of the trap, followed by SIMON and KATE.)*

JACK: And now to find and fight the Giant!

SIMON: Wait for us . . .

(A white flag appears up the trap and waves.)

DAME L: Yooo-hooo!

(It is followed by DAME LANSDOWN, entering up the beanstalk.)

DAME L: *(gasping)* What a climb . . .

SIMON: Talk about high . . .

KATE: We're up above the clouds . . .

DAME L: D'you think I need an oxygen mask?

SIMON: Any sort of mask'd be a help.

DAME L: Cheeky boy . . .

KATE: What a view . . . I can see the Mendips . . .

SIMON: I can see the Cotswolds . . .

JACK: I can see the Chilterns . . .

DAME L: I can see the bloomers . . .

SIMON: The bloomers?

DAME L: Cherie Blair's bloomers – on her washing line.

SIMON: You shouldn't look.

DAME L: You can tell plenty about a person by the pants they peg out.

KATE: The air up here is wonderful. It makes me want to sing . . .

DAME L: *(sitting on a bean pod)* It makes me want to sit down . . .

SIMON: *(sitting)* What we doing up here anyway?

KATE: *(sitting)* We've come to help Jack.

SIMON: But just think of all the things we could be doing if we weren't stuck up this beanstalk . . .

ALL: Such as what?

(LXQ.43; FSQ.16)

SONG: IF I WERE NOT STUCK UP THIS STALK *(To the tune of If I Were Not Upon This Stage, by Tom Sutton) (SIMON, KATE, JACK, DAME LANDSOWN)*

SIMON:
IF I WERE NOT STUCK UP THIS STALK,
SOMETHING ELSE I'D LIKE TO BE.
IF I WERE NOT STUCK UP THIS STALK,
A BOXER I WOULD BE
YOU'D HEAR ME ALL DAY LONG –
SINGING OUT THIS SONG:
(With boxing business.) LEFT JAB – RIGHT JAB –
LEFT JAB – RIGHT JAB
NICE ONE, HARRY. NICE ONE HARRY.
LEFT JAB – RIGHT JAB – LEFT JAB – RIGHT JAB.
NICE ONE HARRY, KNOW WHAT I MEAN?

(FSQ.16A)

KATE: IF I WERE NOT STUCK UP THIS STALK,
SOMETHING ELSE I'D LIKE TO BE.
IF I WERE NOT STUCK UP THIS STALK,
A WAITRESS I WOULD BE
YOU'D HEAR ME ALL DAY LONG –
SINGING OUT THIS SONG:
(Miming plates.) EGG AND CHIPS, EGG AND CHIPS.
TOAD IN THE HOLE,
(Screeching.) ALRIGHT! I'M COMING!
EGG AND CHIPS, EGG AND CHIPS.
TOAD IN THE HOLE,
ALRIGHT! I'M COMING!

(FSQ.16B)

JACK: IF I WERE NOT STUCK UP THIS STALK,
SOMETHING ELSE I'D LIKE TO BE.
IF I WERE NOT STUCK UP THIS STALK,
A FOOTBALLER I'D BE
YOU'D HEAR ME ALL DAY LONG –
SINGING OUT THIS SONG:
(With actions.) BANJAX BECKHAM, CUT ROUND COLE,
TACKLE GIGGS AND SHOOT
AND GOAL!
BANJAX BECKHAM, CUT ROUND COLE,
TACKLE GIGGS AND SHOOT AND GOAL!

(FSQ.16C)

DAME L: IF I WERE NOT STUCK UP THIS STALK,
SOMETHING ELSE I'D LIKE TO BE.
IF I WERE NOT STUCK UP THIS STALK,
A DIVER I WOULD BE
YOU'D HEAR ME ALL DAY LONG –
SINGING OUT THIS SONG:
(Swimming and submerging.) GOING DOWN! GOING DOWN!
BURBLE BURBLE BURBLE
OOPS!
GOING DOWN! GOING DOWN!
BURBLE BURBLE BURBLE
OOPS!

(Each person's mime should almost hit the people next to them but, for instance, SIMON does a knees-bend as KATE swings a plate which would have hit him in the face. The only one who connects is JACK who repeatedly kicks DAME LANSDOWN as she bends over.

Having established all four mimes simultaneously, they repeat at speed before:)

ENSEMBLE: IF WE WERE NOT STUCK UP THIS STALK . . .

BLUNDERBORE: *(off)* FEE FI FO FUM . . . !

ALL: BUT WE ARE!

(They all run off screaming and jerking their actions. Blackout.) ***(LXQ.44; FSQ.16D)***

(FlyQ.6; LXQ.45; SQ.24)

Scene Two

Outside Castle Blunderbore.

The castle walls are solid and forbidding. Buttresses form a "U" shape with three doors each with a trapdoor above. The doors to right and left are not practical but, from the trap above the stage right one, a huge mallet swings out and hits you on the head and, from the trap left, a huge orange glove comes out and Tangoes you. The trap above the centre door slides up to reveal the code.

Smoke and sinister Music, ravens, wind, etc, as JACK and KATE enter warily.

JACK: So this is Blunderbore's castle . . .

KATE: It's jolly huge, forbidding and such a . . . scary sort of place.

JACK: But I mustn't be afraid if I'm to be a hero. I've got to get in there and challenge him to fight.

KATE: But how do we get in?

JACK: It must be one of these doors . . .

KATE: But which one?

(He pulls the handle on the L door. The huge orange glove reaches out through the trap to Tango them but misses.)

JACK: No good. *(They step forward, not seeing the glove.)* There's nothing in there, is there?

AUDIENCE: YES . . . GLOVE . . . *(Etc.)*

KATE: Well we didn't see anything.

JACK: I'll try this one . . . *(He pulls the handle on the door R. The hammer flails out through the trap, just missing them and unseen by them.)* That's locked, too. Nothing there. What?

AUDIENCE: HAMMER . . . MALLET . . . *(Etc.)*

KATE: Well we still didn't see anything.

JACK: Let's try this one. *(Approaching the door C.)* There seems to be some sort of handle . . .

(He pulls the handle. There is the sound of a gong and the panel slides up to reveal the code:)

U– M – PAH
U– M – PAH
STEE KIT
OOP – YOR – U – M – PAH

JACK: It looks like some sort of code – or a magic formula, perhaps.

KATE: But what does it mean?

JACK: Perhaps, if I say it aloud, it'll open the door. Trouble is, I don't read very well.

KATE: Oh crumbs! Neither do I. Will you help us? What d'you think it says?

(The AUDIENCE start to read – messily.)

JACK: No. It's not working.

KATE: We'll have to try it all together . . .

(JACK leads the AUDIENCE into rhythm and accelerating (with percussion accompaniment from the pit). The door suddenly flies open ***(LXQ.46, SQ.25)***

revealing "Quiz-Show" effects of tracers, searchlights and smoke with bells, klaxons, hooters, etc.)

JACK: It worked. Oh thanks, mates. Now for the giant. Come on, Kate!

KATE: See you later.

(They exit, hand in hand into the Castle. The door slams shut. ***(LXQ.47)*** *Eerie Music. SIMON enters R.)*

SIMON: Oooohhh . . . I don't think I like it round here . . . And I've lost the others. Let's go and help Jack, Dame Lansdown said . . . then we got bifurcated in the foliage of the forest and now here I am – on me tod – all alone – outside the giant's castle and I don't know how to get in . . . Plenty of doors . . . Let's see if any of them are unlocked . . .

(He tries the Door L and is Tangoed.)

SIMON: *(enjoying it, ticklish)* Oooh, that was quite nice.

(He goes back for a second helping.)

SIMON: But enough of this. I've got to get in and help Jack. What do I have to do, I wonder? Is there a magic spell or something?

AUDIENCE: OOMPAH . . . *(Etc.)*

SIMON: That's charming, I must say, I –

(The door C flies open with all the effects as before.)

(LXQ.48; SQ.26)

SIMON: You clever kids. Right then. Here we go.

(He exits into the Castle. The door slams shut. ***(LXQ.49)*** *Eerie Music. DAME LANSDOWN enters L.)*

DAME L: So this is Harry Ramsden's. Not a sole in sight – but it's obviously the plaice. Hello? Well, the Lord giveth and the Chinese taketh away.

SIR BEASTLY: *(Off – sings)* "Words fall into rhyme . . ."

DAME L: But soft . . . !

SIR BEASTLY: "Every time I am holding you near . . ."

DAME L: Can it be . . . ?

SIR BEASTLY: "So kiss me, my sweet . . ."

DAME L: I might have known it . . .

SIR BEASTLY: *(appearing round the proscenium DL)* I'm the loveliest knight of the year . . ." *(Advancing.)* Ah, there you are my cheeky cherub. *(Aside.)* Gadzooks but she's hideous and yet – and yet – she's the only woman in the world for me, stap me vitals . . . Letitia! Letitia!

DAME L: Bless you. Bless you.

SIR BEASTLY: You do look hot. Have you been cooking?

DAME L: Cooking? Silly. I've been running.

SIR BEASTLY: Your breath's coming in short pants.

DAME L: Leave my underwear out of this.

SIR BEASTLY: You're too old to run about like that.

DAME L: I'm looking forward to my thirtieth birthday.

SIR BEASTLY: Surely you're facing in the wrong direction. But you look very trim – for a growbag. Are you fit?

DAME L: Fit to drop. I've been getting these terrible muscular pains.

SIR BEASTLY: Really? Where?

DAME L: I'd rather not go into details. But when I take an aspirin, I have to sit on it.

SIR BEASTLY: Did you diet?

DAME L: Green. But it came out all streaky.

SIR BEASTLY: No no. Diet. Diet.

DAME L: I've been on a slimming diet for three weeks. Onions and garlic four times a day.

SIR BEASTLY: Does it work?

DAME L: Believe me, it works everything.

SIR BEASTLY: But have you lost anything?

DAME L: Twelve pounds and all my friends. I had to have my clothes altered. Luckily, this dress is reversible.

SIR BEASTLY: Pity your face isn't. And yet . . . you're the woman I've been looking for – longing for . . . I'faith, me heart is all of a tremor.

DAME L: By my liberty bodice, you know how to get round a girl . . . Why have I almost stopped breathing – breathing? Why is my bosom heaving – heaving? Why is something here inside of me all of a quiver?

SIR BEASTLY: *(offering)* Do you need a hand?

DAME L: Gerroff! Can this be . . . love? Oh, I've never known such bliss. This is so thrilling. My heart is so willing. Oh, Beastly, Beastly . . .

SIR BEASTLY: Letitia, Letitia!

DAME L: Bless you. Bless you.

SIR BEASTLY: I have only one thing to say to you.

DAME L: Oh what is it? What is it? Tell me do!

(Music: Bell note. ***(LXQ.50; FSQ.17)*** *SIR BEASTLY takes her hand and kneels.)*

SIR BEASTLY: *(sings)* TIDDLY WINKY WINKY WINKY
TIDDLY WINKY WOO –
I – LOVE – YOU.
TIDDLY WINKY WINKY WINKY
TIDDLY WINKY WOO –
LOVE – YOU – TRUE.
I LOVE YOU IN THE MORNING
AND I LOVE YOU IN THE NIGHT.
I LOVE YOU IN THE EVENING
WHEN THE STARS ARE SHINING BRIGHT.
SO!
TIDDLY WINKY WINKY WINKY
TIDDLY WINKY WOO –

I – LOVE – YOU! TIDDLY WOO!

DAME L: Oh lawks, Sir Beastly, sir! How you do tease and taunt a maiden so. I haven't twittered so since I was in my teens.

SIR BEASTLY: What a memory!

DAME L: You set me all of a quiver. What can I reply but . . .

(Sings.) TIDDLY WINKY WINKY WINKY
TIDDLY WINKY WOO
I – LOVE – YOU.
TIDDLY WINKY WINKY WINKY
TIDDLY WINKY WOO
LOVE – YOU – TRUE.
I LOVE YOU IN THE MORNING
AND I LOVE YOU IN THE NIGHT.
I LOVE YOU IN THE EVENING
WHEN THE STARS ARE SHINING BRIGHT.
SO!
TIDDLY WINKY WINKY WINKY
TIDDLY WINKY WOO
I – LOVE – YOU!

BOTH: TIDDLY WOO!

(LXQ.51; FSQ.17A)

SIR BEASTLY: Oh, Letitia. You mean as much to me as . . . as my magic beans. There!

DAME L: Beans? That's all you men ever think of. *(To the AUDIENCE.)* Isn't it, girls? Beans beans beans! Harricotts, marrowfats, runners and jumpers. Broad beans, butter beans, soya beans and baked beans. Heinz fifty seven, Cross and Blackwells – Asda's special offer – it's all the same to you . . . You open up our cans and you've got us on toast – with tomato sauce. And then you're off – gone with the wind . . . Rockall, Cromarty, Faroes, Fair Isle – gale force winds in all areas – and what do we get? Totally becalmed . . . and in pod. *(Storming UC.)* Now how do I get into this perishing castle. *(To the AUDIENCE.)* Do you know? Can you help me girls?

AUDIENCE: OOMPAH . . . *(Etc.)*

(The Door C flies open – effects as before.) ***(LXQ.52; SQ.27)***

DAME L: Thank you.

SIR BEASTLY: But, my dear Dame Lansdown . . . Letitia! Letitia!

DAME L: Oh . . . Mange tous to you. And you can put that on your blotting paper and sprout it.

(She exits into the Castle. The door slams shut.)

(LXQ.53)

SIR BEASTLY: *(rushing after her) You'll* regret this! You'll be sorry you spurned me! Ah!

(He is Tangoed.)

SIR BEASTLY: You'll wish you hadn't rejected my advances! Ooh!

(The Mallet hits him on the head.)

SIR BEASTLY: Hell hath no fury like a Beastly scorned . . .

(The Mallet and the Glove attack him simultaneously, beating him to the ground. Blackout.) ***(LXQ.54)***

(FlyQ.7; LXQ.55; SQ.28)

Scene Three

A Corridor in Castle Blunderbore.

All is darkness, save for a faint glow of moonlight. JACK and KATE creep in from L.

KATE: Oh, Jack . . . This is a terrible and terrifying place . . .

JACK: We've got to find the giant.

KATE: I'm sure it's this way . . .

JACK: Or is it that way?

KATE: We've run through such a maze of corridors and passageways, we're completely lost . . . And I'm sure this place is haunted!

(LXQ.56)

(A GHOST flutters on behind her from DR and exits the way it came. They don't see it.)

JACK: Haunted? Don't be daft, Kate! You don't believe in ghosts, do you?

(A GHOST flutters on behind him from DL and exits the way it came. They don't see it.)

KATE: Well . . .

JACK: Well, I don't believe in ghosts! And, any case, we've got our torches. And look – moonlight through the window . . . *(Holding the torch under his chin, he lights up his face as he sings.)*

Song: SILVERY MOON *(KATE, JACK and GHOSTS)*

JACK: BY THE LIGHT – *(Torch off.)*

KATE: *(lighting up her face)* WHAT A FRIGHT OF A NIGHT TO BE IN QUITE A PLIGHT! *(Off.)*

JACK: *(on)* OF THE SILVERY MOON – *(Off.)*

(A Bell tolls.)

KATE: *(on)* EV'RY BUMP – EV'RY CLUMP –
MAKES ME JUMP
IN THIS DUMP! *(Off.)*

JACK: *(on)* I LOVE TO SPOON – *(Off.)*

(A Wolf howls.) ***(SQ.29)***

KATE: *(on)* SOMETHING HOWLED –
SOMETHING GROWLED –
SOMETHING FOUL'S ON THE PROWL! *(Off.)*

JACK: *(on)* TO MY HONEY, I'LL CROON – *(Off.)*

KATE: *(on)* DOOM! *(Off.)*

JACK: *(on)* LOVE'S *(Off.)*

KATE: *(on)* GLOOM! *(Off.)*

JACK: *(on)* TUNE.
HONEYMOON – *(Off.)*

(The Chorus of GHOSTS appear at L and R.) ***(LXQ.56)***

KATE: *(on)* SOMETHING GLARED – SOMETHING STARED –
I DESPAIR AND I'M SCARED! *(Off.)*

JACK: *(on)* KEEP A'SHINING IN JUNE – *(Off.)*

(The GHOSTS rattle chains.) ***(SQ.30)***

KATE: *(on)* IS THAT RAIN OR THE DRAINS –
OR THE RATTLE OF CHAINS? *(Off.)*

JACK: *(on)* YOUR SILVERY BEAMS
WILL LIGHT LOVE'S DREAMS
WE'LL BE CUDDLING SOON – *(Off.)*

(The GHOSTS move closer.)

KATE: *(on)* IT SEEMS EYES ARE GLEAMING
AND SOON I'LL BE SCREAMING! *(Off.)*

BOTH: *(on)* BY THE SILVERY MOON! *(Off.)*

(The GHOSTS dance on to form a line behind them. They all have torches held beneath their chins to light up skeleton faces. The sing the melody.)

GHOSTS: *(on)* BY THE LIGHT – *(Off.)*

JACK & KATE: *(on)* SOMETHING REMINDS ME
THERE'S SOMEONE BEHIND ME! *(Off.)*

GHOSTS: *(on)* OF THE SILVERY MOON – *(Off.)*

JACK & KATE: *(on)* BETTER BE WARY
'COS THIS IS QUITE SCARY! *(Off.)*

GHOSTS: *(on)* WE LOVE TO HOW-W-L! – *(Off.)*

JACK & KATE: *(on)* BY THE MOANS AND THE GROANS
WE GUESS WE'RE NOT ALONE! *(Off.)*

GHOSTS: *(on)* TO OUR HONEY, WE'LL GROWL – *(Off.)*

JACK & KATE: *(on)* BATS! *(Off.)*

GHOSTS: *(on)* SO *(Off.)*

JACK & KATE: *(on)* CATS! *(Off.)*

GHOSTS: *(on)* FOWL.
HONEYMOON – *(Off.)*

JACK & KATE: *(on)* WE MUSTN'T BE DAUNTED
BUT THIS PLACE IS HAUNTED! *(Off.)*

GHOSTS: *(on)* KEEP A'SHINING IN JUNE – *(Off.)*

JACK & KATE: *(on)* IT'S TIME WE GOT RID
OF THESE HORRIBLE KIDS! *(Off)*

GHOSTS: *(on)* YOUR SILVERY BEAMS
WILL LIGHT OUR DREAMS
WE'LL BE HAUNTING YOU SOON – *(Off.)*

JACK & KATE: *(on)* THEY'RE AS WEIRD AS I FEARED
BUT I'LL SOON GET THEM CLEARED!

GHOSTS: *(on)* BY THE SILVERY MOON!

JACK & KATE: BOOO!

(The GHOSTS all scream and run off – pursued by JACK to DR and by KATE to DL. Blackout.) ***(LXQ.57)***

(FlyQ8; LXQ.58)

Scene Four

The Kitchen of Castle Blunderbore.

The back wall is a huge arch with a curtain drawn across it, concealing a corridor. Everything is giant-sized. There is a kitchen range with a grate and huge oven on the wall R. The Magic Hen (puppet) is nestled in a basket on top of the oven with a chute leading from the basket into another basket (down which the golden eggs run). There is a Welsh dresser along the wall L. A huge chair stands LC. It is possible for JACK to climb up onto the chair and from there onto the Welsh dresser. On the dresser is the Magic Harp. Downstage of the dresser is a large pedal bin with the lid open. There is a washing line with giant clothes on it and one end of this hangs down close to the pedal bin.

JACK, with drawn sword, creeps in R.

JACK: Wow . . . ! What an awful place . . . Hey! That must be the magic hen the giant stole from the Squire all those years ago. No wonder the Council Tax is so high and we're so poor. Oh and that poor harp!

(The Harp plays a sad little melody.)

JACK: You must be the magic harp I've heard so much about – that made the people of Cheltenham so happy.

(The Harp plays even more sadly.)

JACK: Don't worry. I'll get you away from here . . .

(The Harp cheers up and plays a jolly tune.)

JACK: Everything's so huge! I hadn't realised the giant was as big as that. *(He climbs up onto the chair.)* He must be . . . massive . . . *(He climbs onto the dresser.)* Must be twice my height – or taller. But I mustn't be afraid . . . *(Sings.)*

(LXQ.59; FSQ.18)

Song: COME ON, JACK
OH DEAR, IT'S HERE, MY CHANCE AT LAST
BUT I'M AGHAST WITH FEAR.
COULD IT BE THAT MY CAREER'S NOT THE HERO'S ROLE?
I'M SO AFRAID I'LL FAIL THE GRADE
WHAT AM I DOING HERE?
AND WHATEVER MADE ME THINK ID REACH MY GOAL.
BUT COME ON, JACK, BE BRAVE!
SHOW YOU CAN BEHAVE
LIKE THE HEROES OF YOUR DREAMS.
YOU MUST PULL YOURSELF TOGETHER,
THERE ARE PEOPLE TO SAVE.
SO NOW HERE GOES! NO FEAR, NO FLAP,
IT'S TIME TO TAP YOUR TOES
AND TO PUNCH OLD BLUNDERBORE RIGHT ON THE NOSE!
(Tap routine and repeat of last two lines.)

(LXQ.60; FSQ.18A)

BLUNDERBORE: *(off UC)* FEE . . . !

JACK: Hang on! Heyup!

BLUNDERBORE: FI . . . !

JACK: *(up onto the chair)* I've woken him up!

BLUNDERBORE: FO . . . !

JACK: *(up onto the dresser)* And he sounds pretty vexed . . .

BLUNDERBORE: FUM!!!!

JACK: *(pointing to the pedal bin)* Ah, there I've spied . . .

BLUNDERBORE: *(sniffing snottily)* I SMELL THE BLOOD OF AN ENGLISH MAN!

JACK: *(sliding down the rope into the bin)* A place to hide!

BLUNDERBORE: BE HE ALIVE . . . OR BE HE DEAD . . .

JACK: And see what happens next! *(He ducks down and slams the lid shut in the nick of time.)*

(The curtain C opens ***(LXQ.61)*** *to reveal GIANT BLUNDERBORE. He is huge and armed with a club.)*

BLUNDERBORE: I'LL GRIND HIS BONES TO MAKE MY BREAD . . . ! *(He sniffs menacingly.)* COULD HAVE SWORN I SMELLED MEAT – ENGLISH MEAT! AH! NOTHING TO EAT BUT . . . BEANS! *(He belches explosively.)* WHOEVER HEARD OF A VEGETARIAN GIANT? *(He prods the Harp with his club.)* HARP! PLAY FOR ME!

(The Harp tries to play but the notes are flat and discordant.)

BLUNDERBORE: HOPELESS! LIKE TFI FRIDAY! *(Prodding the Hen.)* HEN! LAY FOR ME!

(The Hen clucks, ***(SQ.31)*** *flaps and strains and a tiny golden egg rolls down the chute.)*

BLUNDERBORE: PATHETIC! *(Roaring.)* BEASTL-E-E-E!

(SIR BEASTLY enters from UL, carrying a gigantic squeezy bottle with a label saying "Big Fairy" and a huge spoon which he is drying on a gigantic tea towel.)

SIR BEASTLY: *(petulant)* What is it now?

BLUNDERBORE: HAVEN'T YOU FINISHED THAT WASHING UP YET?

SIR BEASTLY: I'm fed up! Look at my hands – washday red – and my chain mail's going rusty! *(He slams the spoon down on the dresser.)*

BLUNDERBORE: SOMETIMES, BEASTLY, YOU SMELL GOOD ENOUGH TO EAT.

(SIR BEASTLY flaps his armpits desperately)

BLUNDERBORE: *(staggering away)* PHAW! I SAID SOMETIMES! *(Sniffs.)* AND YET . . . AND YET . . . I'M SURE I GET A WHIFF OF MEAT. . . ME SNITCH DON'T PLAY ME TRICKS. THERE'S AN ENGLISHMAN IN MY CASTLE.

SIR BEASTLY: I told you, there's a whole bevvy of them come up here.

BLUNDERBORE: THEN FIND 'EM! FETCH 'EM TO ME. THEYLL MAKE A PLEASANT PICNIC 'TIL THAT BEANSTALK'S GROWED STRONG ENOUGH FOR ME TO CLAMBER DOWN AND SET ABOUT THE SLAUGHTER. IN THE MEANTIME, I'M GOING TO HAVE FORTY WINKS – BEEN OUT ALL NIGHT . . . *(Waving his club.)* CLUBBIN'. AND DON'T WAKE ME CLATTERING THOSE DISHES . . . *(He turns to exit UL.)*

SIR BEASTLY: *(drawing the curtain closed as they go out UL)* Alright – Big job!

(LXQ.62)

(JACK lifts the lid of the pedal bin and peers out.)

JACK: All clear. *(Climbing out and crossing to the Hen.)* He's sound asleep. First, I'm going to get some of those eggs *(Picking up the basket of eggs.)* ready to take away. After I beat the giant . . .

(The Harp plays a frantic warning. There is a squeaking off DR – approaching.)

JACK: That must be Sir Beastly coming back. I'd best hide again.

(He puts the basket on the Dresser and dives back into the bin. DAME LANSDOWN enters DR, carrying a handbag, tiptoeing with a squeaky shoe (effect in pit) She stops C, takes an oilcan from her handbag and oils the shoe. She tiptoes on. Now the other shoe squeaks. She oils it. She tiptoes UC, but now both shoes squeak. She takes her shoes off and tiptoes across towards the fire but now her feet squeak.)

DAME L: *(to the Hen)* You look eggsausted. Nobody here. Pssst!

SIMON: *(off DR)* Pssst!

DAME L: } Pssst!
SIMON: } *(off)* Pssst!

DAME L: Will you stop pssting about and come here?

(KATE and SIMON enter furtively.)

KATE: What an awful place.

SIMON: It's not very nice, is it? It reminds me of that awful place on the telly – with Mr Blobby.

(DAME LANSDOWN is bending down to tie her shoe.)

KATE: Crinkly Bottom?

DAME L: *(Starting up)* I have not! Will you stop it, both of you. This is no time for messing about.

KATE: *(tragic – crossing to L of pedal bin)* Oh! Who knows what might have happened to poor Jack?

DAME L: *(tragic – crossing to in front of pedal bin)* Jack! Oh my lovely little ladikins . . . !

SIMON: *(tragic – to Welsh dresser)* Oh Jack. My best mate. Gone for ever . . !

DAME L: *(weeping)* I'll never see my little boy again! *(She sits on the pedal. The lid opens and JACK pops up.)*

JACK: Hello, everybody.

ALL: *(delighted)* JACK!

SIMON: *(taking the sword from JACK)* Hey that's a nice sword, Jack . . . well-wicked.

JACK: Sssshhh!

ALL: *(whisper)* What?

JACK: You'll wake the giant.

ALL: The giant?

JACK: The giant.

ALL: *(loud and scornful)* What giant?

(LXQ.63)

BLUNDERBORE: *(sweeping the curtain aside as he enters – with his club in his right hand and a net in his left)* THIS GIANT! AH! LUNCH! GET 'EM! BEASTL-E-E-E!

(All scream. DAME LANSDOWN and SIMON try to get past the GIANT but he throws the net over them. SIR BEASTLY rushes in, sword drawn, to attack JACK. JACK defends himself with the huge spoon.)

BLUNDERBORE: *(seizing KATE by the wrist)* AH! DESSERT! DELICIOUS!

JACK: Simon! Quick!

SIMON: *(struggling in the net)* What?

JACK: The sword!

SIMON: What?

JACK: The sword!

(SIMON tries to throw the sword to JACK but, being tangled, he muffs it and it falls into the pedal bin. JACK hits BEASTLY on the head with the spoon, stunning him. Then he runs up to the GIANT and jumps on his foot. The GIANT roars and releases KATE. JACK and KATE run off UL.)

BLUNDERBORE: AHHH!

(DAME LANSDOWN and SIMON sink down, netted and exhausted.)

SIR BEASTLY: *(removing the net and helping her up)* Now, my proud beauty . . . Blunderbore, old butty, may I present Dame Letitia Lansdown?

BLUNDERBORE: CHARMED, MADAM. YOU'LL STAY FOR LUNCH?

DAME L: What's on the menu?

BLUNDERBORE: YOU ARE! WITH CHIPS!

DAME L: You wouldn't like me, Mr Pavarotti.

SIMON: And you wouldn't like me . . . He wouldn't like me would he kids?

AUDIENCE: YES.

SIMON: Rotters.

BLUNDERBORE: SILENCE. I'VE GOT SPECIAL PLANS FOR YOU TWO.

DAME L/SIMON: *(quaking)* Ooooohhhh!

SIR BEASTLY: Giant Blunderbore, I crave a boon. You can eat anybody in Cheltenham who makes your mouth water – I crave only the hand in marriage of this . . . beautiful buxom blooming beauty . . . my lovely, luscious, lascivious – Letitia.

BLUNDERBORE: BLESS YOU.

SIR BEASTLY: Call me a romantic, sentimental, boy-at-heart old softie . . .

BLUNDERBORE: I HAVEN'T TIME. BUT, IF THE BAG WILL MARRY YOU, YOU CAN HAVE HER . . .

SIR BEASTLY: *(taking DAME LANSDOWN'S hand)*
The choice is yours, my chickadee.
Cooked to a crisp or married to me.
A trip down the aisle as my blushing bride
Or end up boiled, stewed, grilled or fried!

DAME L: *(wrenching her hand away – heroic)* Heat up the cauldron . . .

SIR BEASTLY: What?

DAME L: Turn the oven to regulo ten . . .

SIR BEASTLY: You can't mean . . . ?

DAME L: I'd rather be marinated than married to you.

SIR BEASTLY: *(wails)* Oh no! My heart is broken! *(Vicious.)* I hate you! I hate you! I hate you!

DAME L: Three hates – twenty-four, four hates – thirty-two . . .

SIR BEASTLY: Curse you, woman. I've only one more thing to say to you . . . *(He bursts into tears.)*

BLUNDERBORE: ENOUGH OF THIS. LET'S GET ON WITH THE PREPARATIONS. BEASTLE-E-E-E!

SIR BEASTLY: Yes Blunders?

BLUNDERBORE: STICK 'EM IN THE COOKER.

(SIR BEASTLY, sobbing, opens the huge oven door, from which smoke and red light pour, ***(LXQ.63)*** *and prods DAME LANSDOWN and SIMON into it, with much wailing and protesting. SIR BEASTLY slams the door.)*

BLUNDERBORE: COME ON, BEASTLY. LET'S GO AND LOOK AT THIS BEANSTALK – PULL YOURSELF TOGETHER MAN . . . THERE ARE MORE FISH IN THE SEA . . .

SIR BEASTLY: *(taking BLUNDERBORE'S hand and being led off UL)* But I wanted a bloater . . .

(LXQ.64)

(We hear the GIANT'S footsteps receding into the distance. ***(SQ.32)*** *A huge door creaks open and slams shut.* ***(SQ.33)*** *JACK and KATE creep in.)*

JACK: Come on, Kate. There doesn't seem to be anybody about . . .

KATE: It's very spooky . . .

JACK: If I can just get my sword, then I can fight the giant . . .

KATE: It fell into the pedal bin – I saw it.

JACK: *(reaching into the bin a retrieving the sword)* Great. I wonder where Mother is?

DAME L: *(in the oven)* Will you get your elbow out of my ear?

SIMON: *(in the oven)* I can't help it. It's only a single casserole.

JACK: They're in here. Mother?

DAME L: Hello?

JACK: What's cooking?

DAME L: I am, you twit.

SIMON: And me, you twit.

DAME L: Now get us out of here.

BOTH: You twit!

JACK: *(struggling with the oven door)* I can't. It's locked. It won't open . . .

(A Flash. ***(PyroQ.7; LXQ.65; FSQ.19)*** *FAIRY BLODWEN appears DR.)*

BLODWEN: Fear not, Jack, I said I'd be back. I'll quickly sort this out.

JACK: Oh. Thank heavens you're here.

KATE: Who're you talking to?

JACK: The Fairy.

KATE: Oh you're not seeing Fairies again. I don't believe in fairies!

BLODWEN: Well that wasn't very nice, boys and girls, was it?
I think it's time I came out of the closet! *(She hits herself on the head with her wand.)* There!

KATE: *(suddenly able to see her, jumps into JACK'S arms)* Ahh! You *are* a Fairy! Do you know anything about cookers?

BLODWEN: There's Aga, Zanussi, Indessit and Creda. Mind, I prefer a double oven and an eye-level grill – so you can get hot fat spat in your eye without having to stoop but . . .

JACK: Never mind all that. Mum's locked in the cooker.

BLODWEN: Piece of cake. There's nothing to it.
Stand well back and watch me do it.

(She flutters to the cooker and waves her wand elaborately. There is a Flash ***(PyroQ.8)*** *and the cooker door bursts open, emitting billows of smoke. DAME LANSDOWN staggers out, wearing a huge roast chicken, she has a tomato and a bayleaf as a hat. SIMON follows, pinioned inside a sausage roll with just his head and lower legs visible.)*

DAME L: I don't know whether I'm a la carte or in the cart . . .

SIMON: I think I'm nearly done . . .

DAME L: Shut up, you silly sausage!

JACK: Come on, Mother . . .

DAME L: Hang on. Hang on. I've just got to sort out this stuffing. *(She gropes behind her and (with a "POP" in the pit) produces a large onion.)* Ooohh . . . I'll never do that to a turkey again!

JACK: Quick. We have to escape and chop down the beanstalk.

KATE: Dame Lansdown. *(Giving it to her.)* You take the hen . . .

DAME L: *(cradling the Hen)* Oh, Jack! This reminds me of when you were a baby . . .

JACK: Simon. You take the harp . . .

SIMON: *(still pinioned)* I can't. I can't . . .

(KATE unvelcros the sausage roll and releases him.)

DAME L: Oh, Simon, do stop messing about!

JACK: Now come on!

(SIR BEASTLY appears DL, sword drawn.)

SIR BEASTLY: What's this? Caught you all. *(Shouting.)* Blunderbore!

(With a roar and waving his club, BLUNDERBORE enters ULC.)

BLUNDERBORE: FEE!

(FSQ.20)

JACK: *(climbing onto the chair)* I'm for you, Blunderbore!

BLUNDERBORE: FI!

JACK: You'll have to deal with me first . . .

BLUNDERBORE: FO!

(SIR BEASTLY herds the others DR while JACK is fighting with BLUNDERBORE, dodging the GIANT'S flailing club. FAIRY BLODWEN is DR leading the AUDIENCE in cheering for JACK. JACK spots the chandelier and blows at it. It flickers ***(LXQ.66)*** *but doesn't go out.)*

BLUNDERBORE: FUM!

JACK: Help me everybody. Quick. Blow.

BLODWEN: Yes, blow everybody. On two three . . . BLOW!

BLUNDERBORE: I'LL SOON SHED THE BLOOD . . .

(The Chandelier flickers.)

BLODWEN: Blow harder. Come on! One two three . . . BLOW!

(The chandelier flickers and goes out, ***(LXQ.67)*** *leaving only the moonlight.)*

BLUNDERBORE: OF AN . . . WHAT'S HE DONE? *(Groping about and flailing.)* WHERE ARE YOU, PIPSQUEAK?

JACK: *(leaping to the ground)* Here, Blunderbore! On guard.

SIR BEASTLY: *(kneeling to DAME LANSDOWN)* Marry me and I'll fight on your side.

DAME L: Oh . . . Alright!

SIR BEASTLY: Oh bliss! *(Turning and joining JACK to fight the GIANT.)* Quick, the rest of you! To the beanstalk!

GOODIES: To the beanstalk!

BLUNDERBORE: FEE!

JACK: You go ahead. I'll stay here and fight the Giant!

BLUNDERBORE: FI!

KATE: But Jack . .

BLUNDERBORE: FO!

JACK: Go! Quickly!

(They exit.)

BLUNDERBORE: *(clubbing SIR BEASTLY)* FUM!

SIR BEASTLY: AH! *(He slides to the floor smiling – zonked.)*

JACK: *(fighting the GIANT alone, shouting)* Simon?

SIMON: *(struggling with the Harp)* What?

JACK: Take Beastly to the beanstalk

SIMON: *(sticks the Harp under one arm and grabs BEASTLY with the other.)* Oh, come on . . . *(He leads BEASTLY off DL.)*

(The GIANT flails with his club but JACK keeps ducking and rolling out of the way. JACK gets under BLUNDERBORE'S guard and stabs him with the sword. The GIANT roars with rage and pain. JACK stabs him again and the GIANT begins to sink, clutching at the cooker.)

DAME L: *(off DL)* Jack! Will you come along at once? I won't tell you again!

JACK: Coming, Mother! Thanks, everybody! *(He runs out DL.)*

BLUNDERBORE: *(staggering and raging)* YOU CAN'T ESCAPE! NONE OF YOU! YOU'LL NEVER ESCAPE!

(Blackout.) ***(LXQ.68; FSQ.19A)***

(FlyQ.9) (LXQ.69)

Scene Five

A Corridor in Castle Blunderbore.

DAME LANSDOWN and KATE stagger on, supporting the semi-conscious SIR BEASTLY.

KATE: Where are we?

SIR BEASTLY: I don't know.

DAME L: You had the guidebook.

SIMON: *(calling from* off *DL)* I've found it.

DAME L: It's alright. This way. Simon's found it.

(There is a toilet flush offstage. ***(SQ.34)*** *Simon enters, looking relieved.)*

DAME L: Well? Where is it?

SIMON: Well I don't know where the little girls' one is but the little boys' one is . . .

DAME L: Not the toilet, you twit – the front door!

SIMON: I know. I know. Follow me. It's . . . THIS WAY . . .

(SIMON runs towards DR but stops and looks puzzled. The others run off DR shouting "IT'S THIS WAY!")

SIMON: *(calling after them)* No it's not. I'm wrong. It's . . . *(Running towards DL.)* THIS WAY . . . !

(The others run back on shouting "IT'S THIS WAY!" and exit DL. SIMON has stopped again.)

SIMON: No. I tell a lie . . . It's . . .

(The others stagger back on, panting.)

SIMON: It's . . . THIS WAY . . . ! *(He leads them to the edge of the stage DR and they all teeter on the edge of the orchestra pit.)*

DAME L: *(grabbing SIMON and shaking him)* Stop it. Stop it. Stop it. Sto pit. sto pit. Pit stop. Pit stop. *(She stops.)* Pit stop? Now think. Concentrate. Which way did we come in?

SIMON: *(infuriatingly slow)* Let's see now – it was a Thursday and . . . No. I tell a lie. It was a Wednesday . . .

DAME L: Get on with it.

SIMON: I was facing that way . . .

BLUNDERBORE: *(off)* FEE! ***(SQ.35)***

JACK: *(running on from DL)* Quick. He's coming . . .

KATE: Hurry up . . .

BLUNDERBORE: *(nearer)* FI! ***(SQ.36)***

SIMON: Then I turned right . . . or was it left?

BLUNDERBORE: *(still nearer)* FO! ***(SQ.37)***

DAME L: Simon . . .

BLUNDERBORE: *(very near)* FUM! ***(SQ.38)***

SIMON: Then I went on a bit and I . . .

SIR BEASTLY: Look out . . . !

(DAME LANSDOWN jumps out of the way just as there is a roar ***(SQ.39)*** *and BLUNDERBORE'S arm swings down from DL, the club hitting the ground where she was standing.)*

SIMON: And then I . . .

DAME L: Oh never mind! Come on!

(They all run off as the GIANT roars ***(SQ.40)*** *and flails again. Blackout.)* ***(LXQ.70) (FlyQ.10)***

(LXQ.71)

Scene Six

DAME LANSDOWN'S Garden. The foot of the beanstalk.

The GOODIES are slithering down.

DAME L: Oh my palpitations. Feel my heart . . .

SIR BEASTLY: Alright then . . .

DAME L: Gerroff!

BLUNDERBORE: *(from above)* I'M COMING DOWN AFTER YOU! ***(SQ.43)***

JACK: He's coming down after us . . .

(The beanstalk starts shaking.)

KATE: Oh corks, Jack. Quickly, Jack. What are we going to do?

(A Flash. ***(PyroQ.9)*** *FAIRY BLODWEN appears DR holding an axe.)*

BLODWEN: Here you are, Jack, take my chopper
And bring the beast a proper cropper.

(JACK takes the axe and chops at the beanstalk. FAIRY BLODWEN leads the AUDIENCE in "ONE! TWO! THREE!" There is a creaking and groaning. ***(SQ.42)*** *JACK chops more. Everybody shouting "Come on, Jack, etc." The beanstalk sways a moment then, slowly at first, tumbles down with a great Crash.* ***(SQ.43; LXQ.72)*** *There is a great scream from above* ***(SQ.44)*** *and BLUNDERBORE (a dummy) falls from the grid* ***(FlyQ.11)*** *to hit the stage with a THUD.)*

ALL: HOORAY!

SIMON: Three cheers for Jack . . .

SQUIRE: Yes indeed. Our very own hero . . .

KATE: You really are a hero now, jack!

JACK: And does that mean that Kate and me can . . . ?

SQUIRE: Egad, lad, you make a Dad's heart glad. Of course you can!

DAME L: That's my boy!

(LXQ.73; FSQ.21)

Song: JACK IS A HERO TODAY *(ALL)*

ALL:
JACK!
IS A HERO TODAY, YOU SEE.
JACK!
WILL GO DOWN IN HISTORY.
HE CLIMBED UP TO BLUNDERBORE
AND BEAT THE GIANT TO THE FLOOR – OH . . .
JACK!
YOU'RE THE LAD WHO IS BRAVE AND TRUE.
JACK!
EVERYBODY HAS FAITH IN YOU.
HE'S THE HERO OF THE DAY
SO LET'S CHEER HIM "HIP-HIP HOORAY!

THREE CHEERS FOR JACK –
OUR LOCAL HERO!
AND WELCOME BACK –
HE KNOWS NO FEAR, OH,
HE'S OUR OWN BOY –
OUR PRIDE AND JOY –
OUR BRAVE AND FEARLESS FAVOURITE LOCAL HERO!

(Blackout.) ***(LXQ.74; FSQ.21A; FlyQ.12)***

(LXQ.75)

Scene Seven

A Clearing in the Woods.

Songsheet with SIMON and DAME LANSDOWN – They have to sing loud enough to bring DAISY back – her favourite song.

WHY DOES A BROWN COW GIVE WHITE MILK
WHEN IT ONLY EATS GREEN GRASS?
THAT'S THE BURNING QUESTION –
BURNS LIKE INDIGESTION –
I LIKE YOU –
YOU LIKE ME –
ISN'T IT A LAUGH?
WHY DOES A BROWN COW GIVE WHITE MILK
WHEN IT ONLY EATS GREEN GRASS?

(KIDS up, messages, etc. Final chorus.)

(LXQ.76; FlyQ.13)

Scene Eight

The SQUIRE'S Ornamental Gardens.

Walkdown.

FINALE *(FULL COMPANY)*

ALL: WHATEVER
FORTUNE MAY HAVE BEEN SENDING,
WE NEVER
DOUBTED THIS HAPPY ENDING.
WE KNEW IT, DIDN'T YOU?
A REWARD FOR LOVE THAT'S TRUE.
PROCLAIM IT –
AND LET NO ONE DOUBT IT,
A SHAME IT –
WOULD BE TO BE WITHOUT IT
FOR LOVE IS ALL
AS YOU MAY RECALL
WHEN THE CURTAIN'S DUE

SIR BEASTLY: LETITIA!
MY DEAR, I REALLY WISH YA
WOULD CONSENT
JUST TO GIVE ME YOUR HAND.

DAME L: IT'S THE WHOLE GIRL
OR IT'S NO GIRL.

SIR BEASTLY: DOES THIS MEAN YOU SAY YEA?

DAME L: OH ALRIGHT THEN – OK.
FETCH ME MY BOUQUET.

ALL: SO NOW WE
WISH YOU WARM SEASON'S GREETINGS
AND HOW WE
HAVE ENJOYED THIS BRIEF MEETING
BUT NOW IT'S TIME
FOR THIS PANTOMIME
TO SAY: "GOOD BYE".

(Curtain.) ***(LXQ.77)***

Props Plot

ACT ONE

Scene One – IN FRONT OF PANTO GAUZE.

Wand for FAIRY BLODWEN – Off DR.
Bag of Magic Beans for SIR BEASTLY – Off DL.

Scene Two – VILLAGE GREEN. OUTSIDE DAME LANSDOWN'S COTTAGE.

Rucksack with big fluffy Bunny for SIMPLE SIMON – Off UL.
Huge Boulder No. 1.
Huge Boulder No. 2.
Huge Boulder No. 3.

The Boulders need to be substantial enough (or floppy enough) not to bounce but mustn't be life-threatening. They could be made of painted foam or from cloth and stuffing sewn up like huge cushions. They can either be dropped from the flies by a trip mechanism or thrown (accurately) from the fly galleries either side.

Milkmaid's yoke with wooden pails for DAME LANSDOWN. One of these has a cat's tail (apparently) sticking out through a knot-hole in the side. This is attached to a modelmaker's electric motor with a switch on the handle of the pail or on the supporting chain – whichever is easiest for the actor to operate it.

A soft (fabric-covered foam) milking stool velcroed onto DAME'S bottom.

Magic Sword. This descends from the flies on fishing line (ideally with a pyro, blazing like a retro, rocket) and is a sort of aerial Excalibur. It can either be attached to a cutout cloud or in a winged scabbard – either way, Jack needs to be able to draw or detach it elegantly.

Large Compass (Alarm clock size) for SIR BEASTLY.
Theodolite on stand – not a real one but a panto version for SIR BEASTLY.
Spade with a sling to be carried like a slung rifle by SIR BEASTLY.
Bag of Magic Beans for SIR BEASTLY.
Dibber on a string to hang from SIR BEASTLY'S belt – this can look a bit rude.
Daisy the Cow – very attractive and lovable.

Inside Daisy:

Bottle of Milk (a dummy one made of latex or similar so as not to break when dropped).
A round metal tray painted purple (Cadbury's Milk Tray colour).
A bottle of Milk Stout (also unbreakable).
One teat contains a squeezy bottle of water to squirt SIMON.

Supermarket Trolley containing:
Milking stool.
Ordinary Metal Bucket (SIMON gets his head, and later his foot, stuck in it).
Huge Scent-spray.
Huge Powder Puff – with powder to send up clouds.
Huge Cotton buds – on either end of a stick about 3' long.
Yellow Duster.
Jeye Cloth.
Wet Hanky in polythene pocket in DAME'S apron.

JOURNEY TRANSFORMATION – (reversible).

Ideally, the COTTAGE trucks off to one side as the hedgerow trucks follow it and the cast mime walking in the opposite direction. The whole change is reversed at speed when JACK, JILL and DAISY run back. When the change is eventually completed, the last hedgerow truck has a post with a sign saying 'Three Miles to Market or "Market – not far". The Backcloth remains unchanged.

Scene Three – THE ROAD TO MARKET.

Bag of Magic Beans.
Crystal Ball (Rubber or soft plastic – silvered) on elastic – for SIR BEASTLY to drop on his foot.

Scene Four – A CLEARING IN THE FOREST (*Front Cloth*).

Bass Marching Drum and beaters for DAME LANSDOWN.
A selection of Trombones, Trumpets, Clarinets, Recorders, Kazoos (whatever people can play) – all pushed on in the Supermarket Trolley.
Huge Gout-Foot for SIR BEASTLY.

Scene Five – INSIDE DAME LANSDOWN'S COTTAGE.

Door off-centre and window centre of the back wall (through which the Dame throws the beans and through which we see the first sprouting of the beanstalk). The curtains should draw on and off when "zapped". High bunk beds L and R with ladders up to them for JACK and SIMON. A large Wardrobe under one of these from which the Dame's bed hinges down with a crash when "zapped".

A Chamber Pot – attached to a pole so that it can shoot out from under the bed and disappear again.
A large old-fashioned wireless set on a shelf.
A wooden chandelier with chintzy shades hanging from the ceiling (or the flies).
A big "Zapper" by which the DAME controls lights, wireless, curtains, bed and chamber pot.
A tiny pyjama top for SIMON.
A Bucket, Glass of Water and large Toothbrush for teeth-cleaning routine.

TRANSFORMATION: The Cottage "BREAKS UP" due to the seismic effects of the growth of the beanstalk – the main parts truck off while others fly out TO REVEAL:

Scene Seven – DAME LANSDOWN'S GARDEN, WITH FULLY GROWN BEANSTALK.

The Beanstalk itself – JACK needs to climb up to sightline – probably about 12 feet.

ACT TWO

Scene One – THE TOP OF THE BEANSTALK. ABOVE THE CLOUDS.

Cloud-top and top-of-the-beanstalk cut-outs augmented by smoke – preferably dry ice.
There are various beanshoots, tendrils and a huge pod (for four people to sit on in a row).
Ideally, the actors will all enter up through a trap as if up the Beanstalk.

Scene Two – OUTSIDE CASTLE BLUNDERBORE.

The castle walls are solid and forbidding. Buttresses form a "U" shape with three doors each with a large handle and a trap door above. The doors to right and left are not practical but, from the trap above the stage right one, a huge mallet (soft) swings out and hits you on the head and, from the trap in the stage left door, a huge orange glove comes out and "Tangoes" you. The trap above the centre door slides up to reveal the code.

Scene Three – A CORRIDOR IN CASTLE BLUNDERBORE. (*Front Cloth*)

Torches for JACK, JILL and the GHOSTS.

Scene Four – THE KITCHEN OF CASTLE BLUNDERBORE.

Everything is giant-sized. The back wall is a huge arch with a curtain drawn across it, concealing a corridor. There is a kitchen range with a grate and huge oven R. The Magic Hen (puppet) is nestled in a basket on a shelf US of the oven with a chute leading from the basket into another basket (down which the golden eggs run) – only two eggs get laid.

There is a Welsh dresser along the wall L. A huge chair stands LC. It is possible for JACK to climb up onto the chair and from there onto the Welsh dresser. On the dresser is the Magic Harp. Downstage of the dresser is a large pedal bin with the lid open. There is a washing line with giant clothes on it and one end of this hangs down (so that JACK can slide down it into the pedal bin – big enough for JACK to hide inside – below).

Basket of Golden Eggs.
Harp – this can be a puppet or part person (costume) and part prop.

For the GIANT: A huge Club (plus a Dagger if he can manage it).
For SIR BEASTLY: Huge Plate, Dish Mop and Washing-up Liquid (possibly labelled "Big Fairy").
Oil Can in large Handbag – for DAME LANSDOWN.
Large Net – which the GIANT (apparently) throws over DAME LANSDOWN and SIMON.
Sword for SIR BEASTLY.
Chicken Costume for DAME LANSDOWN – in Cooker, Necklace of Tomatoes.
Huge Spring Onion.
Sausage Roll Costume for SIMON – in Cooker.

Scene Five – THE SAME CORRIDOR IN THE CASTLE.

Giant's arm with Club to clunk down from behind the proscenium.

Scene Six – DAME LANSDOWN'S GARDEN – THE FOOT OF THE BEANSTALK.

The beanstalk needs to fall so, ideally, this will be a cut-out one which pivots at the base and, controlled from the flies, falls. The top of it is high enough to be masked both when it is vertical and when it is horizontal. Failing all else, the "pull-up" beanstalk can simply drop.

Woodman's Axe for FAIRY BLODWEN – off DR.
Full-sized Dummy (soft) of GIANT BLUNDERBORE which can drop out of the grid. (He could always fall off stage and the actors can follow his trajectory with their eyes).

Scene Eight – A CLEARING IN THE FOREST.

SONGSHEET.

Lighting Plot

ACT ONE

Cue	Effect
1	Light area DL – sinister for SIR BEASTLY.
2	Light area DR – pretty for BLODWEN.
3	Lose DL area.
4	Light tableau – Village behind Gauze.
5	Add full light as Gauze flies out – Sunny day – Opening Number.
6	Build for final chorus.
7	Reduce slightly for "acting light".
8	Brighten for DAME'S entrance.
9	Very colourful (pulsing?) for DAME and VILLAGERS' song.
10	Return to state of LXQ.7.
11	Add light for BLODWEN DR.
12	Very magical and mysterious for "Magic Sword" song.
13	Add bright single beam for sword to "fly" down.
14	Return to state of LXQ.12.
15	Return to state of LXQ.7.
16	Romantic for farewell to DAISY.
17	Return to state of LXQ.7.
18	Romantic for "Side by Side".
19	Return to state of LXQ.7.
20	Snap B.O.
21	Front Cloth – evening.
22	Brighten for scene.
23	Fade to beautiful evening.
24	Instant snap night – romantic.
25	Fade to B.O.
26	Interior of Cottage – night.
27	Light switched on.
28	Light switched off – Moonlight through window.
29	"Magic" light as the Beanstalk begins to grow.
30	Dark, green, sinister as the Cottage breaks up.
31	Green but romantic for the "Bean Ballet".
32	The Garden – night – the Beanstalk fully grown.
33	Add light for BLODWEN DR.
34	Add light for SIR BEASTLY DL.

35 Add dramatic green light down the Beanstalk.
36 Focus more on the Beanstalk as JACK begins to climb.
37 Lose F.O.H. as the Curtain falls, leaving tableau on stage.

ACT TWO

38 Very dramatic – above the clouds (dry ice?) for the RAVEN'S dance.
39 "Acting light" as SIR BEASTLY climbs up.
40 Add light for BLODWEN DR.
41 Return to state of LXQ.38.
42 Return to state of LXQ.39 – but brighter.
43 Colourful for number.
44 Snap B.O.
45 Very eerie and sinister – exterior of Castle Blunderbore.
46 Full "Quiz-show" effects – tracers, searchlights, etc.
47 Return to state of LXQ.45.
48 Full "Quiz-show" effects – tracers, searchlights, etc.
49 Return to state of LXQ.45 – but a little brighter.
50 Very colourful "cod" romatic for DAME/SIR BEASTLY duet.
51 Return to state of LXQ.49.
52 Full "Quiz-show" effects – tracers, searchlights, etc.
53 Return to state of LXQ.49.
54 Snap B.O.
55 Very dark – corridor in the castle – Front Cloth.
56 Add (barely) touch of green cross light for line of GHOSTS.
57 Snap B.O.
58 Very eerie and sinister – the Giant's kitchen – glow of fire – glimmering chandelier
59 Colourful for JACK'S song and dance.
60 Return to state of LXQ.58 .
61 Dramatic for BLUNDERBORE'S entrance.
62 Return to state of LXQ.58 – but brighter.
63 Red light glowing in cooker.
64 Return to state of LXQ.62.
65 Add light for BLODWEN DR.
66 Lights flicker but stay on.
67 Lights go out leaving moonlight.
68 Fade to B.O.
69 Front Cloth – the Corridor – moonlight.
70 Snap B.O.
71 The foot of the Beanstalk – dawn beginning to break.

72 The sun bursts through as the Beanstalk falls.
73 Very bright for celebration song.
74 Snap B.O.
75 Front Cloth – bright for Songsheet.
76 Crossfade to full stage for Walkdown and Finale.
77 Lose F.O.H. as Curtain falls, leaving tableau on stage.

Follow Spot Plot

ACT ONE

Cue	Effect – Stage R Spot	Effect – Stage L Spot
1	Pick up SIR BEASTLY DL.	
2		Pick up FAIRY BLODWEN – DR.
1A	Snap B.O.	
2A		Fade B.O.
3	Pick up KATE & SQUIRE C.	Pick up KATE & SQUIRE C.
3A	Fade B.O.	
4	Pick up KATE C.	Pick up KATE C.
4A	OPEN to include SQUIRE & SIMON.	OPEN to include SQUIRE & SIMON.
4B	Fade B.O.	Fade B.O.
5	Pick up JACK C.	Pick up JACK C.
5A	BOTH OPEN (LETTERBOX) TO INCLUDE KATE, SQUIRE & SIMON.	
5B	Fade B.O.	Fade B.O.
6	Pick up DAME LANSDOWN UR.	Pick up DAME LANSDOWN UR.
6A	Fade B.O.	Fade B.O.
7	Pick up BLODWEN DR.	
7A	Pick up JACK C.	
7B	Fade B.O.	Fade B.O.
8	Pick up DAME, SIMON & DAISY C.	Pick up, DAME, SIMON & DAISY C.
8A	OPEN for JACK and KATE.	OPEN for JACK and KATE.
8B	Fade B.O.	Fade B.O.
9	Pick up JACK/DAISY C.	Pick up KATE/DAISY C.
9A	Snap B.O.	Snap B.O.
10	Pick up KATE C.	Pick up KATE C.
10A	Fade B.O.	Fade B.O.
11	Pick up JACK C.	Pick up KATE C.
11A	Fade B.O.	Fade B.O.
12	BOTH Pick up DAME LANSDOWN'S CROSSOVER IN BAKED BEAN TIN.	
12A	Fade B.O.	Fade B.O.
13	Pick up BLODWEN DR.	Pick up JACK C.
13A	Fade B.O. as Curtain Falls.	Fade B.O. as Curtain Falls.

ACT TWO

14	Pick up SIR BEASTLY C.	
15		Pick up BLODWEN DR.
14A	Fade B.O.	
15A		Fade B.O.
16	Pick up SIMON C.	Pick up SIMON C.
16A	Include KATE.	Include KATE.
16B	Include JACK.	Include JACK.
16C	Include DAME LANSDOWN.	Include DAME LANSDOWN.
16D	Snap B.O.	
17	Pick up DAME LANSDOWN C.	Pick up SIR BEASTLY C.
17A	Fade B.O.	Fade B.O.
18	Pick up JACK C.	Pick up JACK C.
18A	Fade B.O.	
19		Pick up BLODWEN DR.
20	Pick up JACK C.	
19A		Fade B.O.
20A	Fade B.O.	
21	Pick up JACK C.	Pick up JACK C.
21A	Snap B.O.	Snap B.O.
22	BOTH FOLLOW CALLS AND FINALE TO CURTAIN DOWN.	
22A	BOTH FADE B.O. as Curtain Falls.	

Sound Plot

ACT ONE

Cue	Effect
1	Crack of THUNDER.
2	Crack of THUNDER.
3	Crack of THUNDER.
4	**BLUNDERBORE:** "FEE FI FO FUM".
5	Descending SWANEE WHISTLE and TYMPANI thud as Boulder is dropped.
6	**BLUNDERBORE:** Short ROAR.
7	Descending SWANEE WHISTLE and TYMPANI thud as Boulder is dropped.
8	**BLUNDERBORE:** Long ROAR.
9	**BLUNDERBORE:** "FEE FI FO FUM".
10	**BLUNDERBORE:** "BE HE ALIVE OR BE HE DEAD".
11	**BLUNDERBORE:** Short ROAR into descending SWANEE WHISTLE and TYMPANI thud as Boulder is dropped.
12	**BLUNDERBORE:** Long ROAR.
13	**BLUNDERBORE:** Short ROAR.
14	NIGHTINGALE.
15	Clock CHIME.
16	CAT miaows angrily and spits.
17	Disco music.
18	THUNDER Rumble.
19	Creaking of timbers.
20	Creaking, groaning falling masonry – Ripping apart of the Cottage.
21	**BLUNDERBORE:** ROAR ending as a triumphant CHUCKLE.

ACT TWO

22	Crack of THUNDER.
23	Crack of THUNDER.
24	Moaning WIND with caawing Ravens – eerie.
25	Gameshow GONG, BELLS, HORN, KLAXON.
26	Gameshow GONG, BELLS, HORN, KLAXON.
27	Gameshow GONG, BELLS, HORN, KLAXON.
28	Rumble of THUNDER.
29	WOLVES Howl.

30 Rattling of CHAINS.
31 HEN clucks and strains.
32 Receding Giant FOOTSTEPS in echoey corridor – Huge DOOR CREAKS open and SLAMS shut.
33 Bubbling COOKER.
34 Toilet FLUSH.
35 **BLUNDERBORE:** "FEE".
36 **BLUNDERBORE:** "FI".
37 **BLUNDERBORE:** "FO".
38 **BLUNDERBORE:** "FUM".
39 **BLUNDERBORE:** Short ROAR.
40 **BLUNDERBORE:** Long ROAR.
41 **BLUNDERBORE:** "I'M COMING DOWN AFTER YOU".
42 Beanstalk CREAKING.
43 Beanstalk CREAKING and FALLING.
44 **BLUNDERBORE:** DEATH CRY.

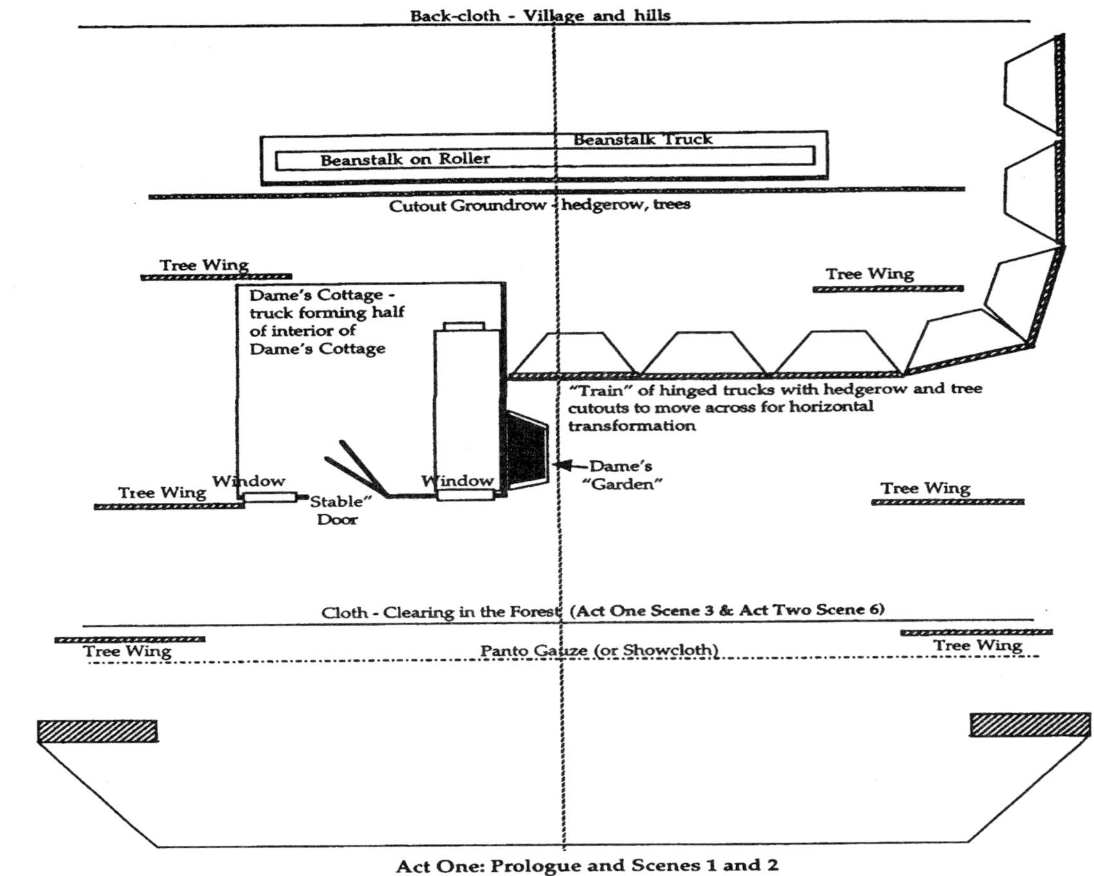

Act One: Prologue and Scenes 1 and 2

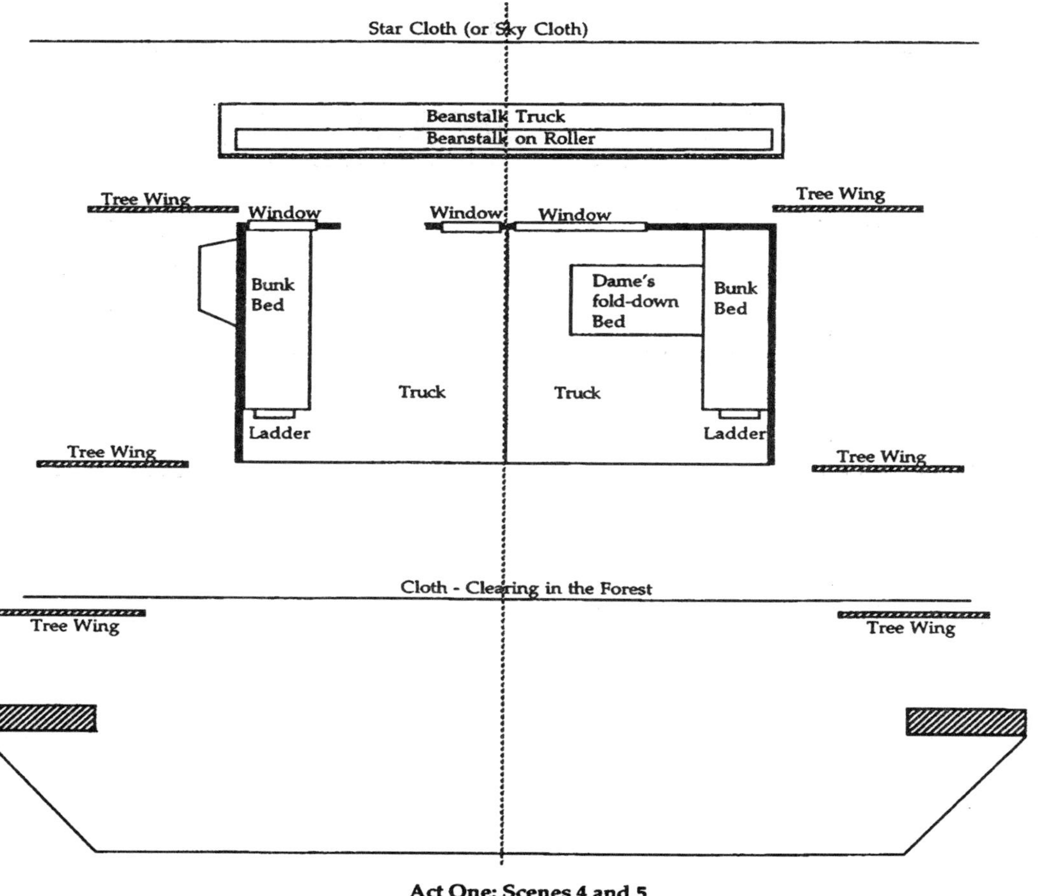

Act One: Scenes 4 and 5

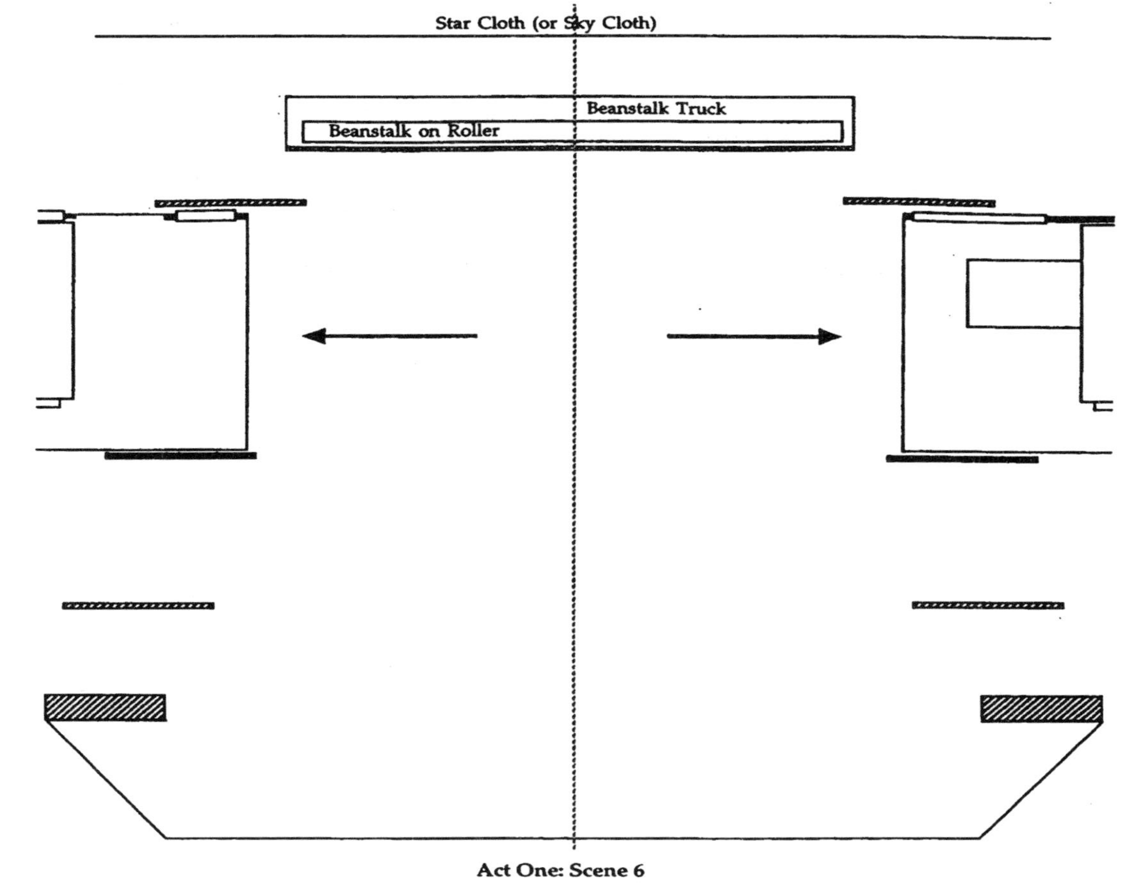

Act One: Scene 6

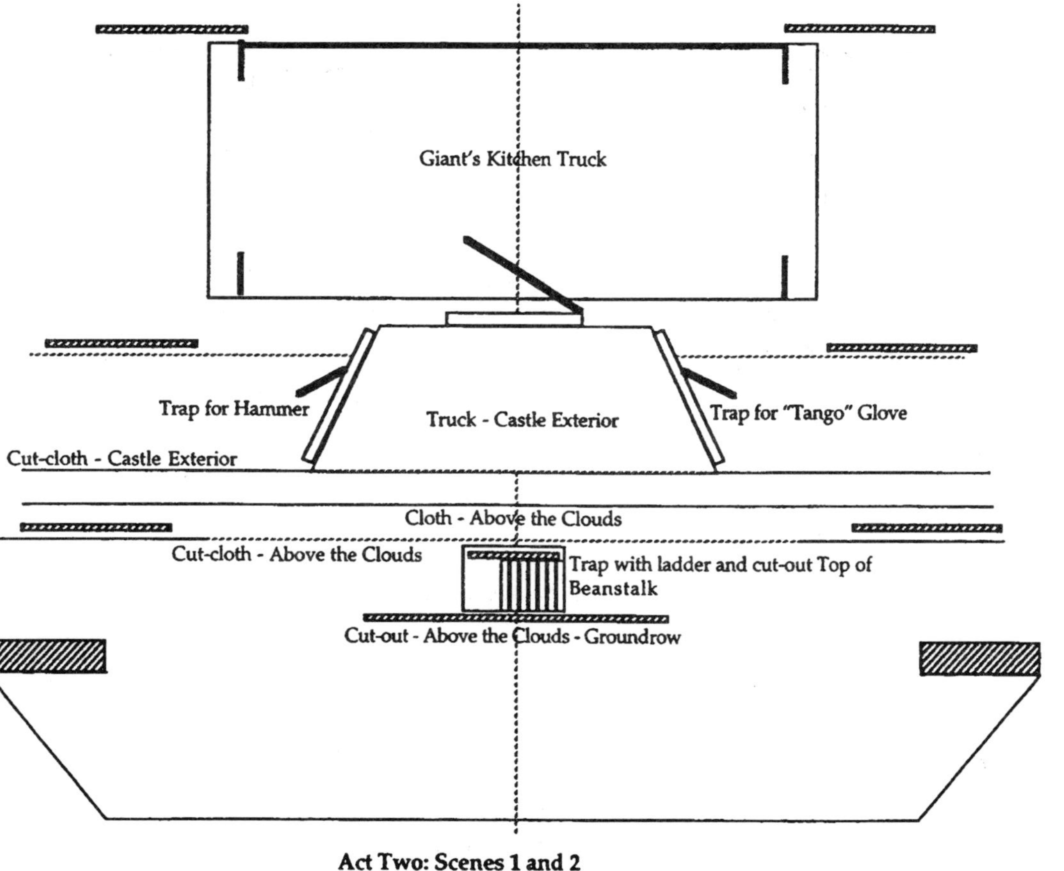

Act Two: Scenes 1 and 2

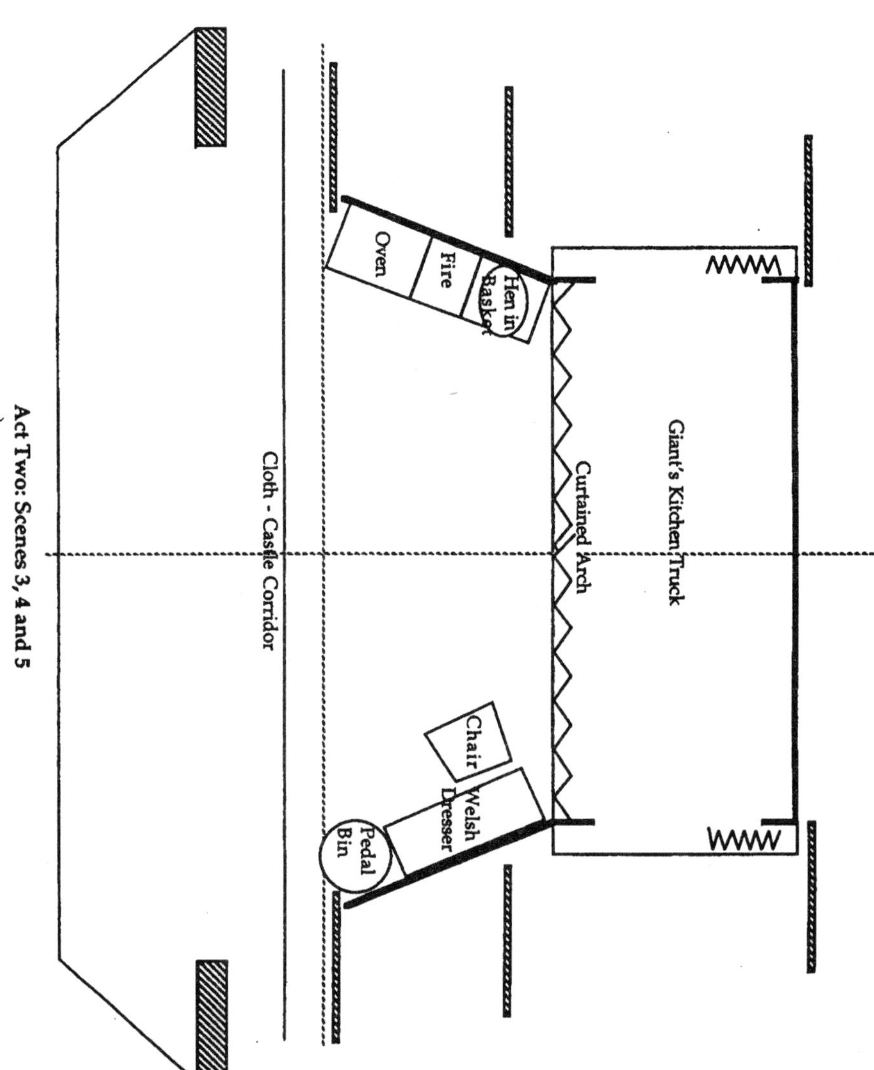

Act Two: Scenes 3, 4 and 5